Healing the Heart

Healing the Heart

Desert Wisdom for a Busy World

Kenneth C. Russell

Layout and design: Gilles Lépine
Cover: "Life of the Desert Fathers" by Starnina. Italian Renaissance tableau.
© 1993 Novalis, Saint Paul University
Editorial office: Novalis, Saint Paul University, 223 Main Street,
Ottawa, Ontario K1S 1C4.
Business office: Novalis, 49 Front Street East, 2nd Floor,
Toronto, Ontario M5E 1B3
Printed in Canada

Canadian Cataloguing in Publication Data

Russell, Kenneth C. (Kenneth Charles), 1934-
    Healing the heart: desert wisdom for a busy world

(Inner journey series)
Includes bibliographical references.
ISBN 2-89088-618-2

    1. Cassian, John, ca. 360 — ca.435. 2. Eremitic
life — Egypt. 3. Deserts — Religious aspects —
Christianity. 4. Asceticism. 5. Spiritual
healing. I. Title. II. Series.

BR1720.C3R88 1993   255'.02   C93-090467-2

NOVALIS

For Denise

Contents

Introduction

With its snakes, scorpions, wild beasts and bandits, the Egyptian desert was not one of the favourite health spas of the well-to-do in the fourth and fifth centuries after Christ. They preferred more comfortable surroundings, a more moderate climate, and the proximity of a healing spring. Thousands of men and a smaller number of women, however, did penetrate the desert for "health" reasons. They went there seeking the tranquillity of mind and body that would enable them to love God and neighbour without hindrance.

To attain this, they put themselves in the care of spiritual masters who taught them how to live the "eremitic" life. These masters encouraged them to reveal their inmost thoughts so that their problems might be diagnosed and proper treatment might be prescribed. It was largely this science of the way to develop a loving heart that made the first practitioners of Western monasticism look on the Egyptian tradition with such admiration. They were eager, therefore, to learn everything they could about it.

This widespread curiosity explains John Cassian's popularity. All kinds of exotic stories about the desert dwellers could be gleaned from the works of travellers, and those who were interested could even consult the collected sayings of the Desert Fathers and Mothers. Yet for a developed exposition of desert wisdom there was no better source than the writings of John Cassian. Cassian, after all, had been there! He hadn't merely passed through on a whirlwind tour like so many others. A monk himself, he had gone to Egypt from his Palestinian monastery to learn what he could from the spiritual masters of his age. He had sat at their feet for approximately a decade, listened to them talk and, what is more important, he had tried to live what they told him. He had an experiential knowledge of their teaching. What he tells us in his *Institutions* and his *Conferences* is filtered through twenty-eight years of monastic practice and is adjusted, as he tells us, to the circumstances of western monks, but this seems to strengthen the trustworthiness of what he says, rather than to detract from its authenticity.

The story of Europe's fascination with Egyptian ascetics has a certain antiquarian interest, but does John Cassian have anything to say to us today? I think he does, because Christ continues to ask his followers "to be perfect as your heavenly Father is perfect" (Matthew 5:48). The men and women who trudged out to the desert took the call to let grace transform them very seriously. What they aimed at was not some sort of psychological well-being, but a complete orientation of all their thoughts and impulses in the direction of love. They proceeded, therefore, to correct everything in them that bore the marks of selfish concupiscence. They wanted to be the new men and women they had set out to be at their baptism. The result of their reflections and practice was a rich psychological and spiritual wisdom. We can learn from them.

Indeed, it seems to me that one cannot afford to neglect this treasure at a time of renewed interest in the contemplative life. Obviously the jewels we find there are in settings that seem dated and strange to us. To recover the insights of these spiritual masters we have to see beyond the particular context of their time and situate the truth they expressed in our own familiar setting.

I believe that Cassian's account of the Desert Fathers' treatment of what he terms "passions" offers a therapeutic approach to spiritual health. I have tried, therefore, to understand what he is saying and to express it in a way that will be helpful to people today. The very notion of "passions," however, illustrates the difficulties we encounter when we pick up an author who wrote centuries ago. The term "passions" means one thing for us and another for John Cassian. By "passions" Cassian means the pressures and inclinations that push us toward a particular pattern of behaviour. Others before him had elaborated theories about the origin of these *logismoi* (persistent streams of thought) which turn us this way and that, but it seems to me that Cassian is very much the pragmatist. He adopts the list that Evagrius Ponticus (d. 399) extracted from the writings of the great theologian Origen (d. 253), but he keeps his attention primarily on the practical problem of dealing with the tendency toward eating disorders, sexual disorders, avarice, anger, sadness, acedia,[1] vanity and pride.

Some of these tendencies he regards as natural, others as unnatural. Some are prompted by internal stirrings, others by external events. Some involve the body, others the mind, and still others both body and mind. In fact, he is describing an existential reality we all experience.

He calls these wayward tendencies "diseases," and the terminology is well chosen. A disease is something we contract; it is not something we manufacture. It is a given of life. But where does it come from? Today we would name nature and environment as its sources. A person has a tendency to overeat—that is, to eat to the detriment of his or her own well-being because of early training, social values, glandular malfunction, and so on.

Cassian likes to expose the full-blown disease in its extreme form, and so he also terms the passions "vices." It is important,

---

1. I have kept this anglicized Latin word because the familiar terms "laziness" and "sloth" do not really describe what the Fathers were talking about.

however, to realize that until the person elects to go with a particular current, as it were, he or she is merely subject to an unhealthy tendency. Sickness, not guilt, is the issue.

People who want to focus on loving God cannot do so in the way they would like as long as they are inclined to react angrily to events or are obsessed with their material security. It is not a matter of learning how to control anger once it arises or how to regulate avarice but of reaching the point where anger and avarice are vanquished altogether. The goal is a purity of heart in which the uncontaminated will is focused fully on God. Cassian avoids the word *apatheia* or passionlessness when he describes this condition because he knows that many people react negatively to this concept. He wisely prefers the purity of heart metaphor which he actually equates with *caritas*. The aim of *apatheia,* according to Cassian, is not to reduce people to emotionless lumps on the landscape. Rather, it is to make them free beings, lovingly and undistractedly fixed on God and neighbour.

As we shall see, Cassian is no great admirer of pure passivity. His aim is to increase the intensity of being, not lessen it. We do him an injustice, too, if we think that his high esteem for the hermit's life implies that his spirituality is turned in upon itself. The fact is that the "passions" are rejected because they turn people away from God and isolate individuals from the concerns of the community. Love, on the contrary, builds community and increases concern for others. Anyone who doubts the warmth of human relations in the desert, or thinks that there was disregard for the body, need only glance at the conclusions and introductions of the various chapters of Cassian's *Conferences* to note how frequently the host is careful to see that his guests are properly fed and that they get enough sleep.

John Cassian wrote his *Institutions* for monks living in community, but the solitary in his cell was never far from his mind. Today, oddly enough, there would seem to be more hermits than there have been for centuries. There is, however, another group of contemplatives who live even more obscure lives than these religious who fight cabin fever in cottages or other out-of-the-way places. I am referring to people from various walks of life who feel called right in the midst of secular life not merely to contemplative prayer but to a lifestyle that gives priority to silence and solitude. Though they may be married and, according to the dominant wisdom, committed to action in the world, they live on the edge of society, shunning involvement in its campaigns and distraction. They are not sanctified, therefore, by their action. They need to be aware of the demands of a more contemplative path. This work is especially addressed to these people, who probably have no access to John Cassian's writings and, in any case, are likely to ignore them, since he seems to have only monks in mind.

Even when he talks about cenobites, or members of religious orders following a communal rule of life, Cassian's tendency to return to the hermit actually makes his teaching perfectly applicable to those whose existence is primarily given over to prayer and solitude, whatever their state of life and its distance from the routines of monasticism. A hermit is, we might say, a do-it-yourself monk, and much that is applicable to the solitary can be applied to others living lives of prayer without the benefit of the monastic regime.

Each chapter of this book draws its material from the respective chapter or "book" of Cassian's *Institutions,* the work in which he lays down the fundamentals of monastic life. He deals with the eight principal "vices" from book 5 to 12. He also deals with them briefly in Conference 5. The *Conferences* convey the wisdom of the desert in instructions or lectures supposedly given by various spiritual masters in answer to questions posed by Cassian and his travelling companion, Germanus.

Since the most nearly complete English translation of Cassian was produced in 1894[2] and the most recent partial

2. Edgar C. S. Gibson, *The Works of John Cassian,* vol. 11 in *A Select Library of the Nicene and Post-Nicene Fathers of the Christian Church,* 2nd series (Oxford: James Parker & Co., 1894). This series was reprinted in 1964 by Eerdmans.

translation into English[3] ignores the material on the passions, I have only rarely quoted Cassian directly. The text is designed to stand alone; however, readers will be greatly enriched if they are able to refer to the somewhat-dated English of the nineteenth-century translation, or to the complete French translation in the *Sources chrétiennes* series published by Cerf,[4] or, even better, to the Latin text which accompanies it.

3.   John Cassian, *Conferences.* Translated by Colm Luibheid. In *The Classics of Western Spirituality* series (New York: Paulist Press, 1985).

4.   Jean Cassien, *Institutions cénobitiques.* Edited by Jean-Claude Guy. Vol. 109 in the *Sources chrétiennes* series (Paris: Cerf, 1965); Jean Cassien, *Conférences.* Edited by E. Pichery. 3 vols.: 1-I-VII; 2-VIII-XVII; 3-XVIII-XXIV (Paris: Cerf, 1955, 1958, 1959), vols. 42, 54, and 64 in the *Sources chrétiennes* series.

1

Disordered Eating

In his analysis of the passions, Cassian follows the diagnostic method which medicine has employed since the time of the ancient Greeks. In his view, each passion is a disease and so, like a skilled physician of his time, he sets out to understand the nature of the illness, its causes, prognosis and cure. He will frequently illustrate the development of a passion with case histories very much in the manner of popular articles on psychology. Sometimes it is obvious that one good story has led to another and taken Cassian off the point altogether. Generally, however, the examples he gives are precise demonstrations of the blindness of human folly.

Cassian begins his study of what we usually call gluttony by giving it a Latinized Greek name, *gastrimargia*, which he interprets as "concupiscence of the gullet," or less literally, "concupiscence of the appetite for food and drink." I suspect that in this case Cassian reaches for a neutral Greek word not simply because he wants to refer back to the list of Evagrius but because he wants to cover as wide a range as possible. He is not concerned with gluttony as such, but with what we would term "eating disorders." Indeed, it might be more accurate to say that he focuses on "disordered eating." This label covers overeating, undereating, fussy eating, not waiting for meal times, and every other activity that gives eating or not eating an emphasis it does not deserve.

Why we eat

To understand Cassian's approach to *gastrimargia* we have to consider the basic and utterly naive question: Why do we eat? Obviously, we eat to live. But there is more to it than that. We eat the way we do because it conforms to our particular notion of what constitutes "good living." We are not interested in merely staying alive. In all but the most desperate circumstances, we want to live what we consider a good life.

Not so long ago, an image of sedentary well-being fostered the ideal of long, heavy meals of many courses, but now, with a different lifestyle and with an emphasis on fitness, we opt for lighter meals. We spend less time at the table and eat foods that promote the alert sense of well-being we enjoy. Both a secretary who sits at a computer all day and a runner preparing to compete in short sprints eat to maintain a good life; given their individual goals, however, they eat quite differently. Yet in each case, right eating or eating properly means that the person eats in such a way that the good life he or she is pursuing is achieved.

Cassian can describe disordered eating because he has a clear notion of what right eating is for the monks he is addressing. A monk is eating the way he should when his eating keeps him alive and promotes the good life he is trying to live.

We shouldn't find it hard to understand the sense of well-being the monks of Cassian's time were trying to cultivate. Like many people today, the monk wanted to have the strength to maintain his regime of prayer and work, but at the same time he wanted to have the alertness he needed to concentrate on prayer and God's word. The key was to eat light. Heavy meals made the monk feel sluggish and distracted at prayer. However, not eating enough to meet the body's needs also interfered with prayer because the monk felt weak and sleepy.

Eating that gets in the way of the good life an individual is trying to live is, in Cassian's opinion, disordered eating. When he is presenting general principles, Cassian emphasizes that the right quantity of food cannot be determined by some objective norm. People differ in age, sex, strength and circumstance. What is too much for a particular individual in a particular place and time may be too little for someone younger, older, or larger, standing right next to him. The norm of right eating is determined, then, by the good life a particular individual is trying to live, and not by a reading on a scale.

Eating is supposed to promote well-being, not sabotage it. When an individual's eating works against him rather than for him, his eating is disordered. It is important to note here that the norm is an individual's conception of the good life. We may regard the meals some social classes ate in the past as unhealthy and, in light of the exploitation they involved, immoral. The participants, however, saw the situation as normal and fell back on the same kind of individual norm Cassian puts forward. We cannot, therefore, use some sort of historical scale to argue that people overate in the past nor, conversely, can we look at the meagre meals of the Desert Fathers and say that they were trying to starve themselves. Objectively speaking, perhaps one group should have eaten less and the other more, but with the obvious exception of those who made food an ultimate good and those who regarded it as an inescapable evil, both groups on the whole ate the way they did because it promoted the good life they valued.

This is an important point in relation to John Cassian's prescription of the way those who wish to live solitary lives focused on God should eat. It is very easy, as we shall see, to be alarmed at how little the desert dwellers ate once we pass from theory to practice. Cassian, in fact, astonishes us by upholding the theoretical norm of eating to promote a good life and then endorsing the highly restrictive diet that was customary in the Egyptian desert. The contradiction is only apparent, however, because Cassian was convinced that historical experience had actually worked out a practical, normative application of the principle. In any case, right eating, not undereating, was what the desert hermits were trying to achieve.

Fasting

The proof of this stands out clearly in the traditional desert teaching on fasting which Cassian hands on. We must make sure, however, that we understand him correctly. Over the centuries fasting has come to mean eating less than we usually do as part of an effort to discipline the body. Nowadays, when our attitude toward the body has been affected by our affirmation of the goodness of the material world, fasting has been reduced to the small measure of self-control in regard to a particular food or the quantity of nourishment consumed. This is certainly a mitigation of even the pre-Vatican II austerity, but fasting remains what it has been for centuries: a matter of reducing the quantity of food eaten. This is not what Cassian means when he speaks of fasting.

Eating less than the body needs during a fast would violate Cassian's principle that the body's needs must be met so that the life of prayer can be maintained. Likewise, eating more than the body needs during a festive season would violate the norm of eating for the sake of the good life. The norm of right eating must be maintained, in season and out of season, as it were. It follows, therefore, that a monk following Cassian's prescriptions would imitate the Egyptian hermits and eat very nearly the same quantity of food on a fast day as on a feast day. Bread constituted the main staple of each meal and, outside of fast days, it seems that a bit of salad or fruit might be added when such things were available.

Cassian himself describes a desert banquet at which the host fed each guest a mouthwatering feast of three olives, five chickpeas, two prunes and one fig in addition to the normal allotment of bread. These extras would be omitted during times of fast, but their absence had very little effect on the amount of food consumed, since the bread ration remained constant. On a fast day, however, a monk ate only once in the evening. This contrasted with the festive days after Easter, when he would eat twice, and with the pattern from September to Lent, when he ate once a day at about three o'clock.

Time, not quantity, distinguished a fast day from an ordinary one. The desert dweller asked himself "When's breakfast?" not "How much should I eat?" While the early monks fasted in accord with the flow of the liturgical year, their motivation was primarily therapeutic rather than penitential. They sought healing, not punishment. John Cassian emphasizes fasting because he sees this as an assurance that rightly ordered eating will be maintained. Fasting is, as it were, the first and elementary therapy for the establishment of peace. I reiterate that, whatever fasting may have become later on, for Cassian it is a health measure, not a punishment.

The downward slope

Although Cassian's list of passions calls to mind the capital sins which scholasticism elaborated, to the hermits in the Egyptian desert they represented the path downward or, in reverse, a therapeutic stairway up to total well-being. Disordered eating leads to sexual disorder, which opens the door, in turn, to avarice, anger, sadness, acedia, vanity and pride in a sort of chain reaction. Some simple souls were convinced that wholeness would inevitably result if you could regulate disordered eating, and thereby block the chain reaction altogether by damming the generation of one vice by another at its very source.

Cassian's understanding of the interconnection of the passions is more sophisticated and realistic. He does see a forward causality at work, especially in relationship to anger, sadness, and acedia, but he is acutely aware that an individual's pacification depends upon the total subjugation of all the passions, and that this cannot be achieved by attacking only one. The linear nature of the list must not be exaggerated. It might be better, actually, to think of the list as a circle. Pride stands at the end of the catalogue of passions, but the list doubles back on itself as the proud individual slips into shameful misdemeanours. The energy flow is not, in fact, only in one direction. All kinds of causal connections exist between the passions. Avarice, for example, promotes anger and breeds acedia. Certainly the list should not be read as a straightforward and complete description of how the passions are interrelated. Those who did read it this way, however, placed great emphasis on fasting because it was the prescribed remedy for *gastrimargia* which stood at the head of the list. They argued that, if a monk could avoid the initial movement downhill which *gastrimargia* represented, he would not have to contend with the other passions which lay below it like the twists and turns of a toboggan slide.

Fasting is only a means

Cassian is quite willing to admit that the struggle against *gastrimargia* is the equivalent of the early, qualifying rounds of the Olympics. If a monk fails here, there is little hope that he will have any success with larger and more difficult opponents. A monk must win this struggle or slide downward. But Cassian insists that winning this battle is not the same thing as winning the war. There is much more to the pacification of the heart than the right ordering of the appetite for food and drink. In fact, Cassian reiterates that, since it is the heart that needs to be set straight, physical asceticism alone will not produce virtue. He drives this home quite emphatically in his treatment of sexual passion, but, even when he speaks of fasting, he insists that a physical fast is useless if it doesn't go hand in hand with abstinence from distractions, anger, and so on.

Cassian refuses to make fasting the be-all and end-all of monastic life. He points out that it is a means toward peace of heart, and not a virtue in its own right. It doesn't follow, therefore, that if fasting until mid-afternoon is good, fasting until the evening of the next day is better. Eating is not an evil to be avoided, and fasting not a goal to be pursued for its own sake.

When fasting is made an end in itself, the result is cruel, silly, and inhuman behaviour, as Cassian's examples show. Monks who exaggerated the importance of fasting, and who perhaps derived considerable satisfaction from the reputation for holiness it gained them, refused to break their fast to join their guests in a meal, as hospitality and Christian love required. Others were unwilling to set their fast aside to join in the festive meals appropriate to the great feast days in the liturgical calendar. Still others stubbornly persevered in their asceticism, even when it was clear that their body needed nourishment. Cassian finds this conduct particularly horrifying and remarks that those who act this way kill the bodies they are supposed to save.

Fasting may not be a virtue, but when it is carried to an extreme, it does take on some of the characteristics of a vice. Not eating enough is as much a violation of the norm of rightly ordered eating as fussy, ill-timed or excessive eating. The norm is to meet the body's needs, but not to feed desire. Monks who turned fasting into a competitive, gymnastic exercise fed their pride and failed to meet their body's needs. As a result, they were oppressed by weakness and fatigue and deprived of the lightness of being required to live a life of prayer. When eating in any quantity or frequency whatsoever becomes the goal of life rather than a means to an end, it seriously interferes with the effort to live a balanced, God-centred life.

Cassian wrote quite sensibly about fasting at a time when some monks, anxious for praise, lied about the severity of the ascetic regime they followed (*Conf.* 18, 7-8) or even discreetly dusted their cheeks with chalk to look emaciated.[1] We have seen that, since monastic life was ascetical, there was a strong temptation to think that, if a little fasting is good, the more severe the fast, the better. In rejecting this idea, Cassian lays down the principles that should govern the eating of those dedicated to a life of prayer. He specifically rejects the idea that fasting is a cure-all act of aggression against the body. Each monk must meet the specific needs of his body according to its

---

1. Irenée Hausherr, *Spiritual Direction in the Early Christian East.* Trans. Anthony P. Gythiel, *Cistercian Studies* series 116 (Kalamazoo, Mich.: Cistercian Publications, 1990), pp. 186-187.

age and condition in this particular place and time. Therefore, no objective norm can be laid down to regulate how much each monk should eat. All of them should follow the monastic calendar which dictates the number and timing of meals at the various seasons, but each individual will have to decide for himself how much he must eat to maintain his vigour and alertness. In every case, however, a monk will rein himself in just this side of satiety.

If we think of diet as a component in a certain lifestyle, we can understand why Cassian wanted monks to eat enough but not too much. Although we may be rather relaxed about our own eating practices, we can appreciate that individuals with very specific life goals must pay more attention to how much they eat than we do. We can even understand that when everything has been stripped away, the egocentric ingestion of the world which eating represents can be a problem for an ascetic. He can quiet or uproot the other passions but he will never be able to escape his appetite for food. It constitutes a highway that can lead him back to the intersection of the other passions, if he wanders down it. The minute eating becomes a pleasure in its own right rather than a pleasure-giving means to live a God-centred life, an individual moves down the road toward avarice, acedia, anger, sadness, and sexual urges.

We certainly have no trouble whatsoever recognizing the validity of the test of love to which Cassian submits every practice. He demonstrates quite convincingly that the failure to love self and neighbour, which is as characteristic of those who overemphasize fasting as it is of those who overeat, is proof positive of the selfish nature of their conduct.

Fasting in the desert

Our sympathy with Cassian's argument for sound eating comes to a sudden end, however, once he turns from general principles to a consideration of historical practice. We are shocked to learn that, after a period of experimentation with various diets, the Desert Fathers settled on a daily ration of two small loaves of bread weighing approximately one pound in all and yielding, I would think, 1000 calories at the very most. One thousand calories is about 1500 under the daily energy intake recommended by modern nutritionists for an adult male! Needless to say, this monotonous diet, lightly supplemented by the odd bit of green vegetable or fruit, hardly conforms to Canada's Food Guide! Our discomfort increases when we learn that the Egyptian monks severely restricted as well the amount of water they drank.

The whole dietary regime is so detrimental to the well-being of the body that the historical practice Cassian presents as normative seems to contradict the flexible general principles he laid down earlier. The opposition between the two is only apparent, however. The tradition of two small loaves *per diem* emerged from the practical application of the principle that the point of eating was to promote the life that the monk was endeavouring to live. The historical norm represents the common experience of most monks: two small loaves kept life on an even keel.

It is interesting to place this measure of nourishment in the context of the time. In "Conference 2," when Abba Moses lays down two small loaves as the traditional daily ration, Cassian's travelling companion Germanus exclaims, "But, we could never eat that much!" Germanus is thinking of a situation where there are special meals in common on the weekend and a fairly regular stream of visitors with whom a host must break bread. Abba Moses is thinking of the basic minimum that will keep a monk going when circumstances deprive him of the extras Germanus has in mind.

It is clear that two small loaves will not constitute a meal to remember. In fact, this diet was so frugal that when evening arrived, monks had a hard time remembering whether they had eaten or not. Long practice had shown, however, that for most individuals this diet was sufficient to keep them going even through lean times.

Cassian's insistence that it is possible to meet the body's needs without crossing over into excess presupposes a rather exact understanding of the body's nutritional requirements.

Cassian seems confident that he has this knowledge. Because of the advance of medical science over the centuries, we have a different view of things. We cannot agree that two small loaves are enough to satisfy the principle that the body's needs must be met.

We do, however, share this principle with Cassian and we must respect his effort to translate it into a practical norm. The diet of the Desert Fathers was inadequate, not because they set out to deprive the body, but because they erred in assessing how its needs should be met. Therefore it is completely illegitimate for us to argue that the meagreness of their diet proves that they harboured an anti-body attitude.

We must also keep in mind that most of the hermits in the deserts of Egypt were hardscrabble peasants whose lot had been lifelong poverty and deprivation. Their notion of how much food was "enough" must surely have differed from our own conception of how much we must eat to satisfy the body's needs. In addition to this, we must remember that their quest for interior quiet made the calmness induced by their limited diet seem a positive gain.

They certainly would not have felt comfortable with the high energy level we associate with vibrant good health, because they would consider this extra vitality looking for an outlet to be proof that they were eating beyond their needs. They were particularly anxious to avoid this charged-up condition because the medical knowledge of the time taught that the production of sperm was in proportion to the nourishment consumed. A monk who ate beyond his basic requirements increased the sexual pressures he experienced and the frequency of nocturnal emissions, which were often accompanied by lascivious dreams and feelings. John Cassian takes the occurrence of sexual temptations as a reliable indicator that a monk is eating more than his basic needs require. The monk, therefore, should cut back a bit on his food.

There is an oddly scientific cast to John Cassian's teaching on the fasting he proposes as a prophylactic and cure for disordered eating. It was influenced, as we have seen, by a precise assessment of the body's needs, an exact notion of how they should be met, and by a biological conception of the relationship between eating and the production of semen. When we separate his fundamental teaching from the medical framework of his time and the actual practice of the desert dwellers, we are left with valid principles which can be helpful to individuals trying to live healthy, prayerful lives, undistractedly focused on God at the edge of things, as it were.

Applying the principles today

What happens, then, when these principles are reread in terms of our modern understanding of the way we should eat? What does it mean, for example, to meet the body's needs without catering to the ego's desires? We are aware, of course, that our eating often has more than a purely utilitarian purpose. In a work world where many of us don't count for much, we take coffee breaks because we want to comfort ourselves with a coffee and a doughnut. It may be rush, rush in the office, but this time is for us! It's not nourishment we need, but the attention to self it represents.

In fact, in the tense world in which we live, food and drink regularly function as non-prescription tranquillizer and ego-strokers. If we add to the popular craze for junk food, the legitimate, occasional quest for a really special meal, and the fellowship aspect of breaking bread together which the Fathers themselves valued, it is obvious that we are not eating just to keep body and soul together. People don't stop in at a tavern on their way home because they are thirsty. Nor do they reach for a bag of potato chips because they are hungry. Even the three-meals-a-day pattern of the West would seem to be dictated more by the desire to calm the self with food than by an intrinsic need. A certain amount of food must be consumed to maintain the body, but there is nothing in the nature of the nutritional process which says that food must be eaten in one, two or three portions. Different cultures have followed different schedules for centuries.

Eating is not a vice, nor is fasting a virtue. There is nothing intrinsically wrong with downing a Coke at midmorning, nor with reaching for a chocolate bar as the afternoon wears on. A couple of friends who seek out an exclusive restaurant are not gluttons just because their interest in food goes beyond practical necessities. Even John Cassian's conception of rightly-ordered eating takes in more than the merely pragmatic. In his works, monks eat the way they do because it promotes the good life they are seeking to live.

Contemplatives in the world, who are attempting to live the same stripped-down life focused solely on the divine as the early monks lived, have embraced an ascetical approach in which there is a clear turning away from self toward God. Although all Christians share the same essential goals, the tenor of their vocation demands that contemplatives structure their lives to serve their calling. For them, there must be nothing but God. As much as is humanly possible, all their pleasure must be found—not in a turning back on self—but in a reaching out toward the Divine. Their eating, therefore, should take on a functional, bare-bones quality which has room, however, for hospitality and the celebration of good fellowship.

How much contemplatives following Cassian's principles of rightly ordered eating will consume will obviously vary from individual to individual. One thing is certain, if they respect his emphasis on meeting the body's needs, their diet will be more diverse and richer in calories than the one John Cassian thought ideal! Jacques Winandy, a modern Desert Father who has been influential in the restoration of the eremitic life in the Church, comments: "The diet should always be balanced, containing enough proteins to provide for the constant rebuilding of the body."[2] He recommends whole wheat bread, cheese, eggs, beans, peas, lentils, fruit, and raw vegetables. He notes that "some will perhaps be surprised at the attention we give to these matters. But the masters of asceticism all recognize the

---

2. Jacques Winandy, *A Manual for Hermits: For the Use of the Hermits of St. John the Baptist* (printed privately, 1964), p. 16.

importance of a sound diet, fully adapted to the needs of con-templative life. Our body and soul act as a unit. What harms one, harms the other. What keeps one in health, supports the other also. To live according to the spirit, in nearness to God, in the peace of heaven; to keep our judgment clear, our thought and feeling pure, we must give the body a nourish-ment that will not debase it or weigh it down (cf. Luke 21:34), a nourishment that will not incite the passions or bring about a state of nervous agitation, restlessness and the need for change. The program we indicate can provide the body with the nourishment it requires."[3]

Winandy's dietary recommendations follow the vege-tarian pattern of monasticism, but in fact each individual's diet will vary according to the seasonal offerings of the local coun-tryside, personal preference, and cultural background.

It makes good sense for contemplatives to eat to meet the body's needs and to restrain the tendency to use food and drink self-indulgently as compensations for the pressures of modern life. But is the traditional monastic pattern of fasting by the clock, as it were, rather than by quantity, something contem-platives should emulate? I must say that, on the basis of Cas-sian's principles and our own knowledge of nutrition, it seems to me that our custom of undertaking a long period of fasting in which the normal intake of food is reduced must, necessar-ily, be seen as detrimental to both health and prayer. Fasting is supposed to promote the "good life," not interfere with it. The point is not to discipline the body, but to reorder the heart. "Timed" fasting, then, seems the only sensible alternative. It meets the body's needs and keeps it alert in prayer.

Anyone who has come home looking forward to a good meal knows how frustrating it is to find the refrigerator empty or to discover that the person who was supposed to prepare dinner has failed to do so. Eating is the most self-centred thing we do, and our anger flares up very quickly if anything inter-feres with it. But much of the irritation we experience when

---

3. Winandy, *A Manual for Hermits,* p. 17.

meals are late or fail to live up to our expectations is not because our body is deprived of the nourishment it needs, but because we are not getting the comfort and consolation our eating habits have led us to expect.

In fact, one could argue that, in the developed countries at least, comfort and consolation play such a strong role in determining how and when we eat that we have grown insensitive to the signals by which the body indicates its needs. Pleasuring the self has become the primary goal, and meeting the body's needs a fortunate by-product. The therapy Cassian presents to those who endeavour to live an ascetic contemplative life attempts to strip away all egocentricity so that the heart may be focused exclusively on God. Eating, therefore, must be a loving act in which the body is cared for, the primary relationship with God is recalled, and the neighbour, if present, is made welcome.

It follows that fasting by the clock will break our dependence on a pattern of eating dictated more by psychological desires than physical needs. In fact, since it should sharpen our "hearing" by silencing the static of our customary behaviour, fasting should increase our sensitivity to our body's requirements.

Is fasting feasible today?

This is all very well and good, but is the long-term fasting John Cassian recommends feasible today? After all, he is not talking about fasting as an occasional exercise, but as a daily pattern of life whose variations are determined primarily by the flow of the liturgical seasons. If we take the Rule of St. Benedict as a guide to the way that the earlier tradition was integrated into Western monasticism, it is obvious that monks did not, strictly speaking, fast all year round: "From holy Easter to Pentecost, the brothers eat at noon and take supper in the evening. Beginning with Pentecost and continuing throughout the summer, the monks fast until mid-afternoon on Wednesday and Friday. . . . On the other days they eat at noon. . . . From the thirteenth of September to the beginning of Lent, they always take their meal in mid-afternoon. Finally, from the beginning of Lent to Easter, they eat toward evening."[4]

On the other hand, if we remember that how they ate was determined by the kind of "good life" they were trying to live, it is obvious that even monastic feasts had something of the fast about them in comparison with the freedom and variety many people in the world enjoyed. The whole regime was austere; fast days were just more austere than others. The wisdom represented by a pattern of eating that is geared to the tenor of the liturgical seasons, and that fully respects the body's needs while serving the contemplative's spiritual aspirations, is likely to appeal to contemplatives who are not living the structured life of religious. Can they follow it?

Let us first consider the regime of two meals *per diem*, which in the Rule of St. Benedict runs from Easter through to September 13th. This hardly qualifies as a fast in the strict sense, since it conforms pretty well to the normal European schedule before the English and New World custom of a substantial morning meal spread to the Continent. It does, however, eliminate snacks, and it surely comes close enough, though the modern custom of eating at noon and in the evening may not conform exactly to the schedule recommended by the ascetics who kept time by the sun.

But what about the real penitential seasons, when monks ate only once a day, either at mid-afternoon or in the evening? This austerity is a wonderful expression of a selfless preoccupation with God, but can we imitate it? Adalbert de Vogüé, a scholarly Benedictine hermit, argues vigorously that we certainly can, provided that we work toward one meal a day very gradually and with great care. He has followed this practice all year long for a long period of time and boasts of the vigour and energy it gives him. Certainly it leaves a good deal of time free for prayer and reading. However, only those who can consume

---

4. *The Rule of St. Benedict in Latin and English with Notes.* Edited by Timothy Fry. (Collegeville, Minn.: The Liturgical Press, 1981), Chapter 41, p. 241.

as much food at one sitting as they now do at two can meet Cassian's requirement that the needs of the body be met.[5]

Cassian thought that he had resolved this problem of quantity by taking the two small loaves of bread that had sustained the desert dwellers as the norm of the basic minimum. Since we know that this isn't enough, we are faced with the problem of eating a sufficient amount of food, but not so much that we end up feeling bloated.

There is the additional problem brought forward by medical science: when the body goes for more than ten hours—and I presume this means ten active hours—without nourishment, it begins to use its stored-up resources to sustain itself. First there is a decline of energy, and then, as it were, the auxiliary motor kicks in and the slump begins to reverse.

Both these problems can be resolved. De Vogüé has pointed out that when someone eats only one meal a day, he or she has to make dinner a leisurely experience in which really nourishing food is consumed.[6] Just the relaxation which this kind of eating requires would do many of us a lot of good in this age of "fast food" and hurried meals. Those who dine alone might prefer to read during their meal, while those who eat with others can make the dinner hour a special social occasion. Taking the time to nourish the body, in a context which feeds the soul, will allow most people who have moved toward this goal very slowly to consume the nourishment they need for a sense of well-being. An adequate diet should also eliminate, or at least minimize, the "low" which troubled the poorly nourished hermits of the Egyptian desert. A very gradual revision of one's eating habits should also bypass the headaches and weak spells that afflict those who undertake a fast without sufficient preparation.

Fasting, however, is a therapeutic technique, not an Olympic event. It should never be allowed to become important in

---

5. Adalbert de Vogüé, *Aimer le jeûne: L'expérience monastique* (Paris: Cerf, 1988), pp. 126-141.

6. A. de Vogüé, *Aimer le jeûne,* p. 14.

its own right. How much one eats and how often is a personal decision. Cassian's insistence on eating in accord with the kind of life one wants to live can certainly be adjusted to a three-meals-a-day routine that seems to have nothing austere about it. Those who do use the traditional wisdom about fasting to break free of the patterns of the world which serve another agenda altogether should keep firmly in mind that, in Cassian's opinion, a fast should be moderate, constant, unspectacular, and flexible. In fact, Cassian makes the test of a balanced attitude toward fasting an individual's readiness to interrupt a fast to welcome a neighbour or to meet the body's evident need of food. Much to the chagrin of those who wanted to exult fasting into a sure-fire formula for the establishment of interior peace, Cassian would have us remember that, despite its importance, it remains merely a technique at the service of love.

2

Sexual Tensions

John Cassian expects many monks to be continent, but few of them to be chaste. In Cassian's scheme of things, the continent are those who have achieved mastery over their sexual appetites, which continue nonetheless to make their presence felt. The chaste, on the other hand, no longer have their focus on God troubled by sexual concupiscence, nor, for that matter, by any other passion. As we read Cassian we have to keep in mind that when he speaks of continence and chastity, he has given his own particular meaning to words we use interchangeably.

Continence is associated with sexual control, but chastity implies much more. It is synonymous, in fact, with the integrity of mind and purity of heart characteristic of an individual rightly ordered toward God in love. What chastity adds to our understanding of this perfect peace is the realization that it cannot be attained until sexual desire follows the other passions in yielding completely to God's love. When that happens, love will reign supreme.

But why is sexual concupiscence the last passion to go? Why should the perfection of love be so tightly related to chastity? John Cassian, who makes it clear that a monk will not be free of the pull of sexual passion as long as anger, avarice, or any other passion has not been radically reordered, never poses this theoretical question. He is satisfied to let the facts of experience substantiate his point. We, however, do wonder about this. Cassian, after all, is not merely saying that sexual passion is the last to go, but that it cannot be quieted until such time as every other passion has been eradicated. Cassian is telling the monks he is addressing that, to be continent, they must gain control of their sexual impulses. Yet they will not be chaste until anger, sadness, acedia, and the other passions have no claim on them.

It is not difficult, I think, to perceive the anthropological theory behind Cassian's conviction that sexual concupiscence will tug at a monk until he has dealt with all the other passions. After all, sexual passion represents the second strongest inclination in human nature. First comes the desire to eat so that the self may continue in existence, and then the desire for sexual intercourse which serves the purpose of continuing the species. In concrete terms, however, sexuality is the force by which an individual establishes a foothold in the world. A monk is a loner. He owns nothing. He's a nobody who does what he's told. But sexuality holds open the possibility of a wife, children, a home, and status in the world. Until a monk is altogether free of concupiscence, the option of being a "somebody" will not have been completely surrendered. Until concupiscence is banished completely, sexual disturbances will continue to disquiet the monk. The option of taking his place in the world will remain open.

Concupiscence versus love

Concupiscence is the opposite of the love of God. *Caritas* is other-directed and essentially relational. The self is found, saved, and sanctified by being lined up, as it were, on God. Concupiscence is essentially self-referential and non-relational. It infects all our drives and diverts them from their proper object, God, and their true purpose, love. The healing process

Cassian describes is a grace-directed reorientation of the whole
human being towards God. When all our impulses serve the
cause of love, the ego can let go of the last worldly power it has
and, at that point, love, rather than concupiscence, becomes
the spontaneous inclination of our whole being.

The chaste are no longer troubled by the ebbs and tides of
sexuality. They remain focused on God whether they are alone
or in a crowd, awake or asleep. Their calmness, however, is not
the feelingless passivity that St. Jerome caricatured when he
said that *apatheia* turned people into stones. Nor is it the result
of some Herculean act of will tightly curbing the flesh. The
chaste are the same in all circumstances, even in relation to
sexual inclinations, because love is the reflex action determining their every response. Although the chaste remain fragile
human beings, they have been transformed by grace to such an
extent that they experience a faint anticipation of the harmony
between mind and body which will characterize the saved at
the resurrection.

A lifeless passivity is not what John Cassian's therapeutic
approach to the passions is aimed to achieve. Indeed, Cassian
takes a positive view of the sexual turmoil which monks have
to struggle against, precisely because it keeps them alert. The
fantasies which flit through a monk's dreams and the inclinations which stir his flesh present challenges which test and
prove him. They help keep him honest. A eunuch can deceive
himself about his spiritual progress and the degree of peace
which he enjoys, but a monk's dreams and inclinations are
constant reminders of just how human and unintegrated he
really is.

He may think he has reached a high level of peace, but then
the time comes for the natural emission of sperm during sleep
and he finds his mind filled with sexual fantasies. In Cassian's
opinion, if he were truly chaste, he would be undisturbed by
sexual desires even when asleep because love, rather than concupiscence, would have become the primary orientation of his
whole being. This conviction that a chaste monk would be the
same whether awake or asleep led John Cassian to pay what

seems to us an extraordinary amount of attention to the phe-
nomenon of nocturnal emission. We must realize, however,
that how a monk experiences this genital event becomes, for
Cassian, a barometer of the climate of his interior life. "Tell me
about your nights and I'll tell you about your days" succinctly
sums up Cassian's teaching.

Nocturnal emissions

The notion that there is some connection between a
monk's conduct during the day and the unconscious reactions
of his body at night would seem to be founded on the idea that
daytime behaviour provokes sexual fantasies, which bring on
the emission of semen during sleep. Cassian was well aware
that the science of his day saw a different interrelationship of
causes. For example, Hippocrates wrote: "Those who have nocturnal emissions have them for the following reason: when the
humour in the body becomes diffused and warmed throughout
– whether through fatigue or some other cause – it produces
foam. As this is secreted, the man sees visions as though he were
having intercourse for the fluid is precisely the same as that
which is emitted in intercourse."[1] Here it is the flow of semen
which produces the images, rather than the other way round.

Ancient medical science thought that the manufacture of
semen paralleled the ingestion of food. Inordinate eating produced an inordinate amount of semen. Physicians thought that
semen was made in the bone marrow or by a transformation of
the blood into semen near the testes.[2] At regular intervals
excess sperm was naturally ejected from the body.

Cassian accepts this scientific explanation, but holds to the
idea that a schedule of nocturnal emission in which the frequency of ejaculation exceeds the norm indicates a disturbance

1. "On Generation," "On the Nature of the Child," "Diseases IV," in
The Hippocratic Treatises. Commentary by Ian M. Lonie. (Berlin/N.Y.:
Walter de Gruyter, 1981), p. 1.

2. *Ibid.;* Galen, *On the Usefulness of the Parts of the Body.* Translated by
Margaret Tallmadge May. (Ithica, N.Y.: Cornell University Press, 1968),
Book 9, 4, p. 432.

in the passions within. Although Cassian mentions that the intervals between the occurrences of nocturnal emission were longer in the Egyptian desert, he lays down once every two months as normal. He tells us that the Fathers credited more frequent eruptions than that to overeating, distractedness, or the snares of the devil.

If food produces semen, then the relationship between overeating and too frequent nocturnal emission is obvious. We have already seen that sexual disturbances were read by monks as a sign that their food intake was exceeding their bodily needs. They were also careful to regulate how much they drank, because erections during sleep were thought to be caused by the pressure of urine collecting in the bladder. Cassian's reasons for connecting nocturnal sexual stimulation and distractedness during the day are also obvious. Daytime distraction admits images and thoughts which run wild in the mind once the monk is asleep.

The devil was blamed for frequent nocturnal emission whenever no other plausible cause could be found. He was especially singled out as the cause whenever repeated occurrences of pollution kept a monk from approaching the Eucharist. Somewhat on the pattern of ritual impurity mentioned in Leviticus 15:16, 31 and 22:3, a monk who had experienced nocturnal pollution the night before the weekly eucharistic celebration refrained from Communion. The odds on this happening were slim, and when it happened often and the elders could find nothing amiss in the victim's life, they saw this as the devil's strategy. Therefore they counselled the monk to receive the eucharist despite the disturbances of the previous night.

Cassian's efforts to determine a normative pattern for the overflow of semen are shaken somewhat by his inadequate understanding of biology. He even has to qualify the important principle which establishes a connection between intemperate eating and sexual intemperance, because some men pay no attention to their diet and yet seldom or never experience nocturnal emission. He must also struggle to justify fasting as a regulatory strategy because many young monks found that, instead of decreasing the frequency of nocturnal emission, fasting increased it. Cassian explains this as the delayed consequence of earlier overeating, or as the devil's efforts to discourage young monks at the beginning of their ascetical training.

Although he lacked a sound, invariable scientific basis for his teaching, Cassian continues to maintain that nocturnal emission is a measure of the degree of peace within. It is not merely, we must note, a measure of *sexual* control. Sexual disturbances during the night remind the continent monk that he is not yet chaste, but they do not necessarily indicate that his problem is sexual.

Cassian seems to take it for granted that the tensions created by the stirring of any passion whatsoever will seek release in the expulsion of semen. All restlessness is channelled in the direction of sexual concupiscence. Therefore, a monk who is troubled by sexual fantasies will have to do more than merely guard his eyes. He will have to look at his whole life, because it may be a bit of anger hidden away in the corner of his psyche that is causing the problem, or perhaps it is his absorption in the hustle and bustle of the day. An unscheduled sexual eruption is like a red light flashing on a control panel: it announces that something is wrong, but it does not indicate exactly what. It is up to the operator to assess the situation and pinpoint the problem.

Concupiscence and asceticism

Cassian regards sexual concupiscence as a psychosomatic reality which serves as a healthy challenge, or, occasionally, as a sobering reminder that we have not yet reached the heights of perfection. He insists that continence is not simply a matter of mind dominating the sinful flesh. The emphasis he puts on this indicates that some people did deal with sexual concupiscence as though they were pure minds endangered by their imprisonment in corrupt bodies.

Cassian stresses that when Christ says that a man who looks on a woman lustfully has already committed adultery, Christ is not condemning the act of seeing. The evil is in the heart, not the eyes. Punishing the body as though it is an evil thing that needs to be kept down, therefore, will not make an individual continent. It might turn him into some sort of proud, ascetic champion, but it will not make him chaste. There can be no purity of heart until grace and hard work have taught the monk humility and patience.

This principle is tremendously important for a sound, therapeutic asceticism. When sexual concupiscence is seen as an exclusively physical problem, asceticism is transformed into punishment. However, when sexual inclinations are tied to the basic orientation of the heart, asceticism becomes a multifaceted reality focused primarily on the spiritual features of humanity. In this regard it is important to keep in mind that Cassian's suggestion that an increase in sexual fantasies be dealt with by a reduction of the amount of food eaten was not prompted by a desire to punish or to put down the body. He gave this advice because he thought that an inordinate amount of sexual turmoil was caused by an excessive amount of sperm, produced in turn by an intake of food greater than the body needed. In his view of things, the pursuit of the good life clearly called for a decrease in rations.

Does John Cassian really think that chastity, as he understands it, is achievable? He does, provided that one is willing to withdraw from society and follow a strict ascetical regime. Those living in society may master their sexual inclinations, but only those who live in solitude can "somehow depart from the flesh while living in the body" (*Institutes,* Bk. 6, 6). Cassian does not say how long it will take for solitaries to become citizens of heaven in the flesh, but he does maintain that "once anyone has withdrawn from idle chatter, dies to anger and worldly concerns, and is content with only two small loaves a day, less than a satisfying quantity of water, and a period of sleep limited to three or, as some maintain, four hours, and does not believe that he will attain perfect chastity by his own

effort or continence but by the mercy of the Lord (since without this trust, the point of all human labour is vain) he should
recognize in no more than six months that it is not something
beyond his abilities." (*Conference* 12, 15.)

Underlying conviction

Cassian's ideas about how sperm is produced and what
importance should be attached to its irregular expulsion hardly
seems relevant to modern contemplatives, especially to those
who are married or female! However, underlying the dated
elements of his thought is the conviction that sexuality is a
psychosomatic reality which is intimately related to the other
drives and impulses of our being. All the tensions stirred up by
anger, worry, or the idle disconnectedness of acedia have sexual
repercussions.

Who can deny the accuracy of Cassian's observation? Nov-
els and movies have endlessly exploited the connection
between bed and board, pride and sexual degradation, a loss of
the sense of life's meaning and sexual mischief. Horrendous
crimes in our own time have underlined the relationship
between anger and sexual violence.

It is very significant, I think, that John Cassian emphasizes
this interaction of the passions. A human being is all of a piece.
Cassian's remarks on the ascetic practices of some monks make
it clear that not everyone shared his views. It was easy to think
of the body and its sexual stirrings as somehow alien to the
inner being, the *me* within. It was easy to put the blame on the
body and to reduce asceticism to an effort to punish the flesh
and keep it in line.

Cassian does not accept this view of human nature. In fact,
he reacts as strongly as he can against it by insisting that sin
flows outward from the heart, and that it is the heart that must
be set right. Sexual concupiscence is not a solitary force which
can be taken on and eliminated in single combat, as it were. It
certainly can be restrained, but real peace can only come when
the other egocentric, non-relational passions which pressure it

have been eliminated. Love must replace concupiscence as the intuitive force directing our every action.

If Cassian thinks that only celibates who become solitaries out of sight of the temptations of the world and its pressures can hope to be chaste, it is not surprising that he sees marriage as a situation in which concupiscence is increased rather than diminished. However, since Cassian never seems to have addressed the issue of how the laity are sanctified, we must be cautious about blackening his name. Certainly, on the whole, his attitude toward sexual inclinations and the body is positive and rather bright. Nowhere, in fact, is the contrast between Cassian's basic optimism and Augustine's sombre outlook more evident.

Broadening Cassian's conception

Chastity is almost impossible to attain in Cassian's view of things because it is, in fact, synonymous with integrity of mind, purity of heart or, to put it simply, holiness. It represents the highest perfection which God's grace can accomplish in a human being here on earth. Since it is rare and difficult, Cassian associates it with the most unselfish, other-directed regime he can imagine: the eremitic life.

In Cassian's opinion, this is the fast-track to the ideal to which all aspire. In the abstract, it may be so. Although Cassian is quite aware that rubbing shoulders with our fellow human beings often sanctifies us by teaching us self-restraint and consideration of our neighbour, he feels that, since the pressures of our common life work against perfect peace, chastity can only be attained in solitude.

Is this true, in reality? I think that Cassian actually sets up a celibate, eremitic ideal of chastity, and then merges ideal and fact so that the solitary life becomes the *only* way truly to realize purity of heart. What this implies is that those who are called to walk what seem to be lesser paths are not, *by and through that very fact*, called to great holiness. Their vocation works against them!

Today we argue that every vocation is from God, and that every way of life contains within it the ways and means to bring those who belong there to the highest sanctity. Saints, it is true, are few, but the fault does not lie with people's failure to choose "higher" vocations. The response to God's will and the readiness to be what he wants an individual to be is always a response to a divine call to holiness.

Chastity, in the sense of purity of heart and integrity of mind is, therefore, available to all. Only the few may attain it, but each state of life is open to it. The paths by which it is reached vary, however, according to the unique calling of each individual. Surely, for example, the community life which Cassian sees as an obstacle to his eremitic ideal of chastity is, for the cenobite or monk, precisely the means through which he moves toward purity of heart. A married woman does not grow holy by turning away from her love of her husband and children, but by riding the crest of that wave toward the God of love. Cassian seems to envision only one route to purity of heart. We think there are many.

Because sexual desire pulls the hermit out of his solitude back into the world, he eradicates his sexual impulses. We have seen, however, that the point is not to free the soul from the body, but to transform concupiscence into love. The "for me," "non-relational" orientation of the self, which is powerfully represented by sexual concupiscence, is reordered into an intuitive response to the other: God and neighbour.

Is the situation of the solitary essentially different from that of the monk in community or the married woman I spoke of earlier? It seems to me that each of them has to learn to love properly. Love must replace concupiscence. This is achieved in different ways. The day-to-day contact with others that is a barrier to a solitary's sanctification is an aid to the monk in community who moves toward purity of heart by learning to love those he deals with in an unselfish way that builds community. Since sexuality is not an evil, there is no sound reason why using it in the proper context rather than laying it aside (as does the hermit or the cenobite) should not promote holiness.

Here again, something that threatens to destroy the vocation of the hermit advances the married person's fidelity to God. The same genital sexuality which would destroy the hermit's union with God and tear the cenobite away from his community, founds the family and helps draw the couple not only closer together but closer to God. My point is that purity of heart is not necessarily a matter of moving away from the pressures of society nor the use of sexuality but of faithfully exploiting the basic elements of each particular vocation. The means are different but the goal is identical: the implantation of love where the compulsions of the passions once held sway.

3

Avarice

Avarice is usually defined as the inordinate love of money. We all need to pay some attention to amassing the wherewithal to provide for our needs. But some people get so caught up in the process that an insatiable cupidity, the desire to possess, becomes the mode of their existence. Every few years we read in the newspaper that some individual who died of hunger in a rented room or froze to death in an alleyway had a horde of cash or folders of stocks and bonds squirrelled away some place. Money, which is supposed to support life, had become its meaning. When acquisition becomes the whole point of gain, spending is the equivalent of letting something precious tumble out through a hole in the bottom of a bag. To the greedy, money is far too good a thing to barter away lightly. Some may exchange their dollars and cents for works of art or property, which bear the same relationship to cash as stocks and bonds, but getting and holding onto gains is what life is about.

This is the classic, popular notion of avarice which conjures up the picture of a greedy king sitting in his counting house caressing the gold and silver coins heaped around him. It is not, however, what Cassian means by greed. He offers a starker definition of avarice. He defines it, not as an inordinate love of money, but as "love of money," pure and simple.

An unnatural sin

The concept of avarice we are used to working with makes greed an extension of the perfectly natural desire to provide for our own needs. Cassian, on the contrary, regards avarice as an *unnatural* sin which has no grounding in the instinctual inclinations of our being. He sees it, moreover, as a miserable stance taken by a corrupt and slothful mind which is afraid fully to commit itself to God.

The avaricious monk is afraid that the ground will give way below his feet. He refuses to entrust his own well-being to the community. He joins it, but he keeps his options open, nonetheless. He worries about what will become of him when he's old or how he'll manage if he's sick. The poverty of the community makes him think that he should set something aside to clothe himself, and a little extra, just in case the time comes for him to move on. The way in which avarice separates the monk from the community makes its sinful, non-relational nature obvious.

It is an unnatural sin, in Cassian's view of things, because it rejects the economic factors relative to a specific way of life. The monastic vocation is a call to a viable lifestyle: it maintains the body as well as the soul. It is natural to live the life, to do the work that is demanded, and to share in the fruits that result from it. This provides the clothing, shelter, and daily food that the monk needs. Avarice sabotages the monk's fundamental vocational commitment by making the security that should follow from the communal pattern of life into a primary and thoroughly private goal. The aim of avarice, however, is not the maintenance of a standard of living suitable for monks. An avaricious monk does not entrust himself to the community, but neither does he entrust himself to God. His money is not just a supplement to raise him above the vicissitudes of the community's economic history—it is a stockpile to protect him from the downturns of Divine Providence.

The avaricious do not literally love money for its own sake. They love it because it gives them control and independence. It keeps them safe from outside interference. They don't need anybody. They have their ticket out of the community hidden away, so they don't need the community and, though they might never say it right out, they are striving as hard as they can to reach a point where they won't need God. The rejection of God is written into their refusal to trust themselves to be supported by the life to which he has called them. It is vividly expressed by the insatiable thirst for gain which controls their existence. They must work, work, work to acquire money, take precautions to safeguard it, worry about multiplying it, and, above all, since what they acquire is never enough to guarantee their security, they must make sure they never spend it.

If the real goal of the avaricious is to walk safely through time, no amount of money is ever enough. No stockpile of cash is ever high enough to take the place of an infinite God. No human being can ever lay a secure scaffolding over the existential abyss. No man can be his own Providence. Of course, the irony is that no amount of money can ever pacify the anxiety which the avaricious person feels, and thus the miserliness that this imbalance creates makes him perfectly miserable. He is caught in a mathematical discrepancy, so that the coins that should be the means to a better life are turned into an end in themselves. The means of life become life's very meaning.

Since the money he earns by the work that quickly takes over every moment of his day must not be spent but hoarded, the avaricious monk aggressively insists on getting his share of what the community distributes to its members. His possessiveness makes him jealous of others, while his feeling that he can take off any time he likes makes him contemptuous of those in authority and disruptive of the community's harmony.

In a sense, he is not in the community because his money allows him to distance himself psychologically from it, but, at the same time, his greed keeps him from pulling away from it altogether. Therefore, he lives a kind of uncommitted life which bears the same relationship to the full-scale listless disconnectedness of acedia as HIV does to AIDS: having the one, the other must inevitably follow.

Root of evil

Avarice easily turns the monk into a discontented, angry, jealous, insolent, and listless deceiver, who is likely to get involved with all kinds of shady characters in his efforts to multiply his wealth. In light of this, it is not surprising that some regarded avarice as the root of all evil (1 Timothy 6:10). For Cassian, this sin which destroyed Judas is very serious indeed, but he emphasizes that, though it is almost impossible to cure, it is very easy to avoid. It originates, we might say, in an initial failure to commit oneself to the monastic life lock, stock, and barrel. The slightest holding back gives avarice a chance to flourish. In some hidden corner of their being, the rich want what they once had or have never completely given up, while the poor secretly yearn for what they have never had.

In the chapter on avarice in his *Institutions,* Cassian follows his custom of describing a "worst case" scenario. He is well aware, however, that avarice does not usually go so far, nor, for that matter, does it appear so clearly. Some, for example, hide their greed by trying to turn their vice into a virtue, and arguing that it is better to give than to receive. They justify their concern for money with the excuse that they can use their wealth to aid the poor. Cassian ridicules this argument which so blatantly contradicts the poverty to which Christ calls the monk. He is equally critical of those who suffer from a kind of indirect avarice through the pride they take in the wealth of their family.

In John Cassian's view, avarice is not the wild, uncontrolled growth of something natural. Essentially it is the product of a vocational maladjustment caused by a lack of faith. It is an impossible effort to combine the irreconcilable. The avaricious monk surrenders his wealth, and hangs on to it; he joins the community, but stands apart from it; he entrusts himself to God's providential care, but attempts to provide for his own well-being.

Cassian thinks that avarice is easily avoided, because all that is demanded of the monk is a wholehearted commitment to the "givens" of monastic life. The monastic regime provides for a standard of living compatible with the purpose for which it exists. If you really want to be a monk, you accept the whole package, as it were. Cassian points to the example of the senator Syncletius, whose decision to become a monk but not give up all his wealth was derided because it left him neither a monk nor a senator.

Avarice is fundamentally a refusal to entrust oneself to God in the place and state to which one has been called (Hebrews 13:5). The avaricious are like novice swimmers, who pretend to float but keep touching the bottom with the toes of one foot because they do not really trust the buoyancy of the water to support them. In the contours of the particular vocation to which they have been called, the avaricious are overwhelmed by existential anxiety. And just as a mother indicates the basic trustworthiness of reality when she consoles her troubled child by saying "It's all right! It's all right!", so the worries of the avaricious about food, clothing, and old age are only ciphers for their perception of the radical insecurity of life itself. It is the Ground of Being who cannot be trusted. Therefore, they must erect a new god in his place, a god made of materials closer to home. In consequence, avarice ends in a perverse adoration that tradition has not hesitated to call idolatry (Colossians 3:5).

Contemplatives in a consumer society

Clearly, in the industrial nations of the world, material possessions have assumed the role that the traditional indicators of social status once played in more rigidly structured societies. We establish who we are and where we stand in the order of things by the houses we buy, the cars we drive, and the vacations we take. All of this is abbreviated by our statement of where we work and what we do. Who we are, in short, is intimately linked to the economic system, which roughly sorts us out into various classes and economic groupings.

It is not surprising that, in such a system, anxiety about who they are and what they are for drives some people to conspicuous consumption. They attempt to hide their inner emptiness by the solidity of the possessions that surround them. Nor is it surprising that, in a system whose very existence depends upon manufacturing and selling, an exaggerated emphasis on possessions becomes so common as to be accepted as normal.

How, then, do contemplatives live in the midst of a prosperous society? Most, I suppose, will be impressed by Christ's call to be poor and endeavour to witness to the *something more* that a materialistic society can easily forget. But finally, what is the norm of the poverty they assume? How little is "just enough," and how much is excessive?

If we draw on what Cassian says about avarice, we can conclude that the proper standard of living is one that meets the needs of an individual's fundamental vocation. A cenobite, or monk in community, has certain material needs. These foster the worship of God and the well-being of the community. Below a certain standard, the community cannot function well. When material possessions increase beyond need, they hinder the attainment of the community's goals. The accumulation of excess wealth opens the road to avarice. Ever so gradually, the basis of trust switches from God's providential care to confidence in the community's stockpile of resources.

It seems to me that the vocational standard Cassian sets up for the cenobitic monks he is addressing applies to every way of life and is applicable to every period of time. However, the way in which particular individuals live it out will vary in the same way as the application of the norm of eating varies from one person to the other and from one century to the next. Here, as with food, money is supposed to support the good life, not interfere with it. Certainly, it should not define it!

A married couple with children will exploit the opportunities they have to pursue their vision of a good life. They are not out to impress their neighbours with their money nor are they interested in giving a conspicuous example of poverty. Money is the means, not the norm. In a world gone mad with possessiveness, utilizing money in the service of a clear goal is itself a witness to poverty. The ways in which this ideal is lived out will vary endlessly, depending on the economic situation, cultural factors, education, and so on.

The cenobite and the hermit are privileged to be called to patterns of life which can be completely shaped to the demands of prayer. Contemplatives who find themselves called to marriage must often shape their life to meet the obligations of family life and let silence and solitude become dominant only gradually as the complexion of family life changes. Obviously, a married couple with children must make the good of the family the economic standard by which they direct their affairs until the children have left home. Then, however, the couple's fulfilment of their vocation to prayer becomes primary, and their economic life must be shaped to suit that target. The absence of flexibility at this point could well indicate an inappropriate reliance on material possessions.

I would argue that Christ's summons to poverty is addressed to every Christian. No one can anxiously cling to the illusion that money is going to keep him safe and, at the same time, profess perfect trust in God. Poverty – whatever the wealth and prosperity of an individual – involves what the biblical scholar Walther Eichrodt termed "readiness for obedient decision."[1] In other words, poverty implies a readiness to make whatever adjustments are necessary to respond to God's call to pursue the good life. At one moment that might mean that the married couple have a large house, a van, a fabulous sound system, and bicycles all over the place. Later they may strip down to a modest apartment and a simple lifestyle which allows them time alone and time for prayer. There is, in short, nothing wrong with possessing things and nothing wrong with

---

1. Walther Eichrodt, *Man in the Old Testament*. Translated by K & R. Gregor Smith. (London: SCM Press, 1951), p. 26.

having almost nothing, provided that, in each case, the economic status serves the vocation to which God has called an individual. Being poor means that life, not possessiveness or the desire to distinguish ourselves from our neighbours, dictates what we own.

Avarice, according to John Cassian, is not an inordinate love of money: it is love of money, pure and simple. He advises us, therefore, to love the life to which we have been called, and it seems to me that he invites us to embrace the economic factors which are part and parcel of it. They are not a problem unless an existential anxiety, a basic refusal to trust that God's love will hold us up, drives us to attempt to be our own providence. Nothing could be sillier, and no passion is more easily avoided. Once contracted, however, greed is very hard to cure. The avaricious fool, after all, says in his heart, "There is no God."

4

Anger

Anger is a perfect illustration of what Cassian means by the word "passion." Anger is an aggressive, self-assertive, vindictive force which seems to rise up out of nowhere when things are not the way the ego thinks they should be. It spontaneously sets a whole pattern of behaviour in motion. It seems to take us over. It may start small and seem to be completely under the control of reason, but, before we know it, the one wrong that provoked us in the first place has become a whole litany of past injustices and our anger has run out of control. Like a tidal wave, it carries us forward on a destructive path which can wreak havoc on people, property, and relationships. It can, in short, make us "mad." Anger, as I have described it, is an impulsive reaction of the non-relating egocentric self which reacts to any challenge to its effort to order the world to suit its own purposes with an indignant: "How dare you!"

Anger is not purely defensive. It does not merely stir us to protect our own rights and property and the rights and dignity of others. There is an aggressive element in it which wants to punish the offender. Anger can be seen, in fact, as a puny attempt to dispense retributive justice. But we are not God and, more often than not, anger violates the harmony of the community.

Modern psychology, however, has given us a rather different view of anger. We tend to see it as a legitimate incentive toward self-assertion and as a force which pushes us to confront injustice. We want people to be aware of wrongs and stirred up enough to do something about them. We want them to "give a damn!" Without some measure of anger, nothing will get done. The same law seems to apply on the individual level where the very establishment of the self requires a degree of assertion. People who are incapable of anger are weak, emotionally defective human beings.

Is anger ever justified?

Unfortunately, Cassian never explicitly deals with the inevitable need to correct wrongdoers forcefully and "angrily." He does, however, offer the example of the justice of God. The recipient of God's correction may well feel that God is angry, but in fact the smarting the victim feels is not an indication of a disturbance in God himself. This faintly suggests that what passes for anger may be a useful tool in the hands of a superior, but Cassian does not consider this possibility. His objections to authentic anger apply, however, to all situations. Inasmuch as anger is a spontaneous rush of emotion which asserts the self over and against others, Cassian sees it as a force which blinds an individual. It clouds the clear perception of the facts and it perverts judgment.

To those like Augustine, who argue that there are righteous reasons for anger, Cassian responds by pointing out that a small disk held up in front of the eyes blocks out the sun. The effect is the same whether the disk be made of lead, silver, or gold. In Cassian's opinion, anger always confuses reason, regardless of the quality of the argument which prompts it. With St. James he firmly believes that "a man's anger does not fulfil God's justice" (James 1:20). He is also convinced that everyone is quite ready to argue that his or her anger is righteous and reasonable. Cassian finds this completely unacceptable. There is simply no such thing as legitimate and justified anger in his scheme of things.

He delights, therefore, in ridiculing the arguments put forward by those who want to use the examples of divine wrath in the Old Testament to justify their own exercise of anger. He carries their acceptance of anthropomorphism to the extreme to demonstrate how silly it is to imply that God experiences anger. Pushed far enough, literal belief in the metaphors of scripture would oblige us to think that God's excessive drinking occasionally plunges him into a deep sleep. Oddly enough, Cassian never alludes to the far more powerful and pertinent example of Christ's expulsion of the moneychangers from the temple (John 2:13-16).

There is no doubt in Cassian's mind that anger has no place whatsoever in the life of a monk. He is not just saying that it is a bad thing to *show* anger. He knows very well that sometimes the best thing a monk can do is to hold back until the anger that has risen up inside him has subsided. Often prudence and social convention force individuals to bite their tongues. For Cassian, however, real virtue goes beyond social etiquette and elementary morality to the complete eradication of anger toward others.

If anger always clouds the mind and alienates one person from another, it has no proper social function. A brother who feels he must correct another's fault will do a much better job of removing the speck from his neighbour's eye if his own vision is not blocked by the plank that anger puts in his own (Luke 6:41-42).

Purpose

What, then, is anger for? It seems to be instinctive, but if it always hinders action, what purpose does it serve? Why did God insert it into human nature? Cassian argues that anger does exist for a reason and that it does have a proper object. He describes anger as a kind of interior shame which reacts against the lewd, ridiculous thoughts that caper in the mind. It can even legitimately be a reaction against the anger that rises up against the neighbour. The only acceptable object of anger, in short, is the self. For Cassian, anger is an irritation which prompts us to correct the thoughts and inclinations of the heart which, though hidden from men, are visible to God and the angels.

Although we sometimes hear an individual exclaim "I could kick myself!", most anger is directed outward toward others. When anger rises up inside us, we feel a vindictive urge, even though we may not act on it. Cassian is well aware that anger unexpressed is not necessarily anger that has been allowed to dissipate. If we hold our peace and refuse to be swept along by anger, it will eventually evaporate like fog. But we can also choose to hold on to it and feed it in the secret recesses of our being. Just because fear or the lack of opportunity keeps us from openly expressing the fury we feel, this does not mean that anger has been side-tracked. As Cassian points out, in this case anger accomplishes its purpose by creating a coldness between individuals. Angry outbursts or vindictive actions certainly alienate others, but anger in and of itself splits the unity between God and neighbour.

Barrier to prayer

In arguing that anger has no place in the life of a monk Cassian places great emphasis on Christ's instructions in Matthew 5:23-24: "If you bring your gift to the altar and there recall that your brother has anything against you, leave your gift at the altar, go first to be reconciled with your brother, and then come and offer your gift." It is not just a matter of remembering that you wronged someone and getting yourself straight with him before appearing before God. Christ demands that, if "*your brother* has anything against *you*," it is up to *you* to seek to alleviate his discontent. If he feels hurt and blames you, you have to do what you can to heal the division. The issue here is not who is in the right and who is in the wrong, but the need to be reconciled with the neighbour. Until the members of the community stand together, there is something inappropriate about standing before God in prayer.

If we cannot love the neighbour whom we see, how can we love God whom we do not see? If we do not love the neighbour

God loves, how can we be united with God in love? Anger violates the community established by love. It replaces the "we" of the united group with the "I" of the non-relating self. It tries to by-pass the unbreakable link between love of God and love of neighbour. It cannot be done.

A monk, therefore, cannot pray, or, as the scripture puts it, "offer his gifts," as long as he is separated from a neighbour. In effect, anger on his part or sadness on the part of the person with whom he has had a disagreement incapacitates him. His function, after all, is to pray always, and he cannot offer acceptable prayer while he is alienated from his brother.

Escape to the desert

But people are so irritating! Some monks thought that if they could just get away from people, they would be all right! Cassian emphasizes that the desert will not resolve the problems of those who cannot achieve moral maturity in the midst of their community. A hermit may have less provocation than a cenobite, but anger put on the inactive list is merely anger that has been pushed out of sight. Cassian notes, moreover, that dormant vices seem to grow stronger in the desert where the restraining influence of the community is absent. They are merely waiting for the occasion to burst out in full vigour. The solitary can even end up blasting away at inanimate objects. Cassian tells us that he found himself angrily cursing an inadequate pen, a dull knife and an unresponsive flint when he was alone in his desert cell.

Kicking a stone out of our way or slamming down a can opener that refuses to work does not alienate the neighbour. While the action is certainly not very important in itself, it does expose the "offended majesty" aspect of anger. The dominating, world-ordering self has been frustrated and umbrage has been taken. As insignificant as the incident may seem, the individual has been shown to be an irritable person who is not thoroughly at peace with the world. This does not fit the picture of a perfect human being. Cassian says, in fact, that anyone who attains purity of heart and tranquillity of mind will be at peace not only with other people but even with the wild beasts.

Evaluation

If "he who hates his brother is a murderer" (1 John 3:15), anger must be eradicated and not merely repressed. Hatred which we are unable to express either out of prudence or fear, is hatred still. Cassian's target, therefore, is the very rise and rush of the emotion which sets us apart from our neighbour and prepares us to take aggressive action. He suggests that the way to curb this spontaneous response of the disordered self is to realize that, since anger in every and all cases clouds judgment, it must always be rejected. It seems to me that the strategy is like the parental ploy of ignoring the temper tantrums of a two-year-old. When the child realizes that his or her emotional outbursts are not going to change anything, the child abandons this particular power play. Cassian seems to prescribe the repeated reining in of anger on the principle that by-passing it again and again will weaken anger to the point where it becomes inoperative. Since it is never used or encouraged, it simply shrivels up.

Cassian's conviction that sin is any willful act that alienates one person from another forces him to see any and all anger aimed at the neighbour as the expression of a moral sickness that is deeply rooted in our egocentricity. He does not see the angry feeling that sweeps over us when we are provoked as sinful in itself, but he does believe that it originates in a disorder which we have not dealt with and that it is oriented toward sin. He is absolutely sure that this disruptive, self-assertive, vindictive force has no public role to play in the life of those who aim at purity of heart and tranquillity of mind. He does not explain how the evils of the world are to be set right, but the answer, I think, is obvious: love, not concupiscence, is the great force for reform. Those whose spontaneous response is love rather than anger will have the other-directed clarity of mind to correct injustices.

There is a beautiful, paradisiacal quality about Cassian's portrait of a wise man whose judgment is undisturbed by the violent impulses of anger, but Cassian's explanation of the purpose of anger leaves the modern reader unsatisfied. The outward, other-directed nature of anger seems too obvious to be denied. Cassian's effort to argue that anger has an inner, self-critical role seems forced and unconvincing. If anger is, indeed, a force which is meant to play a beneficial role in human affairs, then it should be utilized by reason and not ignored as Cassian advises. Certainly experience indicates that, when anger is kept in check, it does play a healthy role in legitimate self-assertion and in the defence of rights, persons, and goals. We cannot really care about something and rise completely above anger when the object of our concern is threatened. Nor can we make a space for ourselves in society without firmly but calmly pushing against others. Anger is an instinctive, outward-directed force which has been implanted in our nature for a purpose. Unfortunately, Cassian's explanation of that purpose seems inadequate.

Although we cannot wholly accept Cassian's explanation of anger, his argument does make us aware that our anger is very likely to be contaminated by our self-assertive aggressiveness. The anger-driven positions we righteously assume may not be as reasonable as we think! Certainly, when we are angry we do not see things as they really are. We see things as they *feel* to the offended self. This explains why anger that seems to be justified often rages out of control and does more harm than good. The very least that we can take from Cassian, therefore, is a reminder that anger must be read with a sort of rational Geiger counter before it is acted upon. It must be made an instrument of love rather than love's rival.

5

Sadness

In the lists of vices drawn up by those who followed Cassian, sadness and acedia were often lumped together under one or the other term. Gregory the Great (d. 604) dropped acedia and kept sadness, while Hugo of St. Victor (d. 1141) preferred to keep acedia and to let sadness disappear from the list. Cassian himself does note the affinity between the two vices, and includes some of the symptoms that are said to be typical of sadness in the description of acedia. Nonetheless, he describes them separately as two diseases with different causes and remedies.

Cassian describes sadness as a pernicious vice which bites into us, takes hold, and gnaws away at our heart. It unsettles us so much that we cannot pray and leaves us so restless that we cannot quiet our mind enough to read. Everything irritates us: the people we have to live with, the work we have to do, the religious observances we have to attend, even our best friends and the things which usually give us pleasure. The bitterness which rises up inside us seems to sour everything in life. Cassian notes that in this "down in the dumps" state of mind we cannot contribute to the building up of the Church and the community. We are, after all, off in a corner feeling sorry for ourselves. Like all the passions, sadness separates the individual from the group.

Causes

The depression which sends us into a tailspin can be brought on, Cassian observes, by the disappointments we meet in life, by the anger we are forced to pen up inside us, or by the frustrations associated with avarice. If I am busy trying to increase my stockpile of cash, I am bound to run into fluctuations in the market that will upset my plans and defeat my hopes. If I am prone to anger, there are sure to be situations where I will have to swallow my feelings and where I will be tempted to let my fury simmer until anger can throw off the gloom of sadness and show its true colours. Even without these weaknesses, however, I will be subject to injury, insult, and injustice. I can no more pass through the vicissitudes of life without being knocked about than a ship can cross the ocean without feeling the force of the waves.

Sometimes, however, sadness seems to flood over us for no reason whatsoever. Some sunny mornings we wake up in a deep funk that makes no sense at all. Although Cassian offers no explanation of this sadness which becomes a chronic condition in some people, he is aware of its existence. In fact, he takes this sadness which does not seem to be provoked by external events or identifiable moral shortcomings as proof that the germ of sadness is within us. It is sitting there, just waiting for some excuse to flare up. Obviously, sometimes it doesn't bother to wait. The fundamental cause of sadness, in other words, is some inner maladjustment and not what happens to us. Cassian notes that it is not the sight of a beautiful woman that causes lust in a monk but his own lack of a pure heart. Sadness, too, is an inner lack that opens an individual to "the slings and arrows of outrageous fortune."

Oddly enough, Cassian never explicitly identifies the seed of sadness hidden in our heart. However, on the basis of the constant awareness of future fulfilment which he proposes as a remedy, we may argue that the fundamental cause of sadness is the disappointment of the would-be imperial self with the way things are. If the cure for the disease is to keep one's eye on the ultimate fulfilment to be attained in God, then sadness may be said to be caused by a loss of perspective, brought on by exaggerating the importance of something particular and temporal or by the weakening of the magnetic pull of hope on the horizon. If we go slightly beyond Cassian, we may blame this loss of forward thrust either on the individual's failure to cultivate hope or on traumatic experiences in childhood which were so overwhelming that they darkened the perception of the light drawing humanity forward.

Sadness is essentially a stalling in the temporal. It is a slackening of the forward thrust which gives meaning to life. It is a loss of perspective or a "de-eternalization" which drowns the individual in the miseries, discomforts, and disappointments of the present.

If the germ of sadness is within, the disease will not be cured by avoiding people. The sad sack cringing in the corner of his cave is not going to find joy in his isolation. His flight, as Cassian notes, merely changes the scene of his misery. To conquer sadness, the afflicted monk would have to cultivate patience which means, in effect, that he would have calmly to accept the facts of his life and persevere in hope.

Purpose

Does sadness have a positive role to play in the life of a spiritually healthy individual? Cassian believes that sadness is properly provoked by regret for our sins, our yearning for a perfection which continually eludes us, and by our desire for a beatitude which is not yet ours. Therefore, discontent seems to be written into the human condition. It is the product of the distance between the ideal and what is. It can lead to frustration when it prompts an individual to concentrate on the present, but, when the goal of future fulfilment is kept clearly in mind, this sadness makes a person obedient, affable, humble and, above all, patient. There is an optimism written into this sadness which is of the "I'm not there yet, but I'm on my way" variety.

Cassian observes that there is a detestable variety of sadness — what we would term an acute species — which so discourages an individual about the lack of fulfilment in the here and now that it causes despair. In this situation there is no perspective at all. The person is impatient, hard, hateful, and desperate. Life as it is becomes intolerable.

Sadness can be a thin morning mist or a dense haze blocking out the sun. Cassian recommends a rather Stoic strategy for keeping the fog from rolling in. He thinks that the only way to maintain our equilibrium in the ups and downs of life is to keep our eyes fixed on our future hope. Without this, we lose the sense of who we are and where we are going.

Relevance

Though we may have a more sophisticated understanding of how sadness can burrow into our psyches, it seems to me that Cassian's treatment of sadness is still instructive. Without a forward thrust, we do "bog down" in the present and lose our sense of proportion. There is no better strategy than to keep our eyes firmly fixed on the light on the horizon and to avoid the temptation to go off by ourselves when we feel "low." Modern psychology, however, has developed techniques to uncover the hidden causes of chronic and apparently causeless depression. It would be foolish to ignore these aids which can make the thrust forward easier by freeing the individual of the dead weight of the past.

It is interesting to note, in fact, a certain parallel between John Cassian's analysis of sadness and the description of depression offered by the psychoanalyst William Gaylin: "What is important to realize is that depression can be precipitated by the loss or removal of anything that the individual overvalues in terms of his own security. To the extent that one's sense of well-being, safety, or security is dependent on love, money, social position, power, drugs, or obsessional defences — to that extent one will be threatened by its loss. When the reliance is preponderant, the individual despairs of survival and gives up. It is that despair which has been called depression."[1]

Cassian's brief study of sadness vividly demonstrates the all-inclusive nature of the spiritual therapy that he is proposing. It reaches out to heal the whole being. It is concerned with the physical, psychological, and spiritual dimensions of the individual. Everything that can be known about the human being can be integrated into the thrust of this therapy toward God. This suggests an interesting integration of elements which we customarily assign to separate disciplines. If the relationship with God is the key to the meaning of our existence, then getting ourselves straight with God should be the basis of our well-being. This orientation toward God, therefore, should be the norm integrating all the other helping disciplines which keep us physically and psychologically sound. If we take Cassian's approach seriously, we have to conclude that spiritual direction should offer real healing and not merely "guidance."

1. *The Meaning of Despair: Psychoanalytic Contributions to the Understanding of Depression.* Edited by William Gaylin. (New York: Science House, 1969), p. 390.

6

Acedia

Acedia infiltrated the hermit's hut at high noon, when the day had dragged on forever and he felt that dinnertime, which was still several hours off, would never come. Solitaries who contracted the disease came down with a listless, highly infectious, low-level depression that made them discontent with their cell, their work, and the brethren who surrounded them. Everything became simply too much! The nervous agitation short-circuiting their powers of concentration made it impossible for them to focus on any task for very long. They would sit down to read, but the words dissolved into incomprehensible squiggles which they lacked the energy to decode. Everything bored them. Even the people they were usually delighted to see were just another irritation to dodge as quickly as possible. Obviously, with everything feeling as dry as the dust that surrounded them, it was only a matter of time before their discomfort made them wonder why they were wasting their talents in the desert. Surely there had to be more to life than this!

The restlessness that kept the hermit from really getting down to anything made some monks sleepy and led others to leave their cells in the pursuit of good works that needed doing. Why, they reasoned, sit around bored when there are brethren to visit, relatives to check on, and religious women who need help? Let's do something to shake off this lethargy!

Cassian notes, however, that what they thought were remedies only increased the symptoms of the disease. The weary slept longer and the restless seekers after distraction found they needed larger and more frequent doses of diversion to distract them from the emptiness within. They were on such a compulsive treadmill that the externalization in which they sought relief became the major focus of their existence. They were absent from their cell so often that they gradually forgot why they had been there in the first place. Even when they did stay home, they spent all their time waiting for meal time and checking for visitors.

Acedia is still with us

I have described acedia as a virus that flourished once upon a time in the Egyptian desert. The truth is that acedia is with us still. Anyone who has worked in an office has met the time-server whose life is measured out in coffee breaks and long lunch hours. Once you have encountered one of these sluggish characters whose life seems an endless flurry of activity that never really produces anything, then Cassian's story of an idler who decides to take action against an earnest young monk rings true. The young monk's energy and output is likely to increase the daily quota of work, so the slothful monk exploits the young man's enthusiasm for excellence to convince him that they should secretly take off to another monastery, where the level of spirituality is higher. At the last moment, of course, the older monk leaves him in the lurch. Since the young man who has been played for a fool is too embarrassed to return to the community, the idler can continue his unproductive life undisturbed.

This story of a fifth-century "gold brick" explains why acedia was renamed "sloth" when the list of what eventually came to be called "capital sins" moved out of the monastic setting into the world of negligent clerics and slugabed lay people. One of the symptoms of the disease, in effect, was taken for the disease itself. We find it hard, however, to think of laziness as a major vice. We are inclined to view the lackadaisical attitude of slackers with benign amusement or to explain it as the consequence of psychological problems or social conditioning. However, a hint that there is more to this vice than meets the eye is implied by the way we continue to label it with the rather esoteric term, "sloth."

Cassian not only tells the story of the monk who wants to work as little as possible, but he writes at some length about the value of manual labour. He does not, however, identify acedia with laziness. "Accidics" may be lazy, but that is not the root of their affliction. It is important, I think, to leave the notion of laziness aside in order to get to the essence of acedia, because, whatever we call this affliction, it is not merely a disease that flourished long ago in a distant place, as I noted earlier. It is with us still, and I suspect that milder versions of it are as frequent as the common cold. It strikes anywhere and anyone. Even today, however, its special target is the contemplative who has taken up a position at the edge of society in order to be alone with God. To discover acedia's true nature we must take a more careful look at John Cassian's treatment of this passion.

Fighting the infection

Cassian ridicules the idea that one can spin out of the range of the Noonday Demon on a whirligig of distractions. He insists, on the contrary, that the only way to fight this infection is to stay put and stick it out. He adds one more important element: the hermit must work. We must keep in mind that we are a long way from the intellectual traditions of Cassiodorus's Vivarium, a sixth-century monastic house of learning, and the medieval *scriptoria,* where erudite monks produced beautiful manuscripts. Although John Cassian himself is a writer, when he refers to work he means daily, monotonous, sweat-producing manual labour.

Cassian insists that a monk must work. The Egyptian tradition required monks to earn their daily bread. Normally they would do this by braiding ropes or weaving baskets that were bought up by wholesalers and sold in the market. The monks would also hire themselves out during the harvest season so as to have enough money to meet their own needs and something left over to offer the poor. Cassian greatly values this economic perspective, as we shall see, but his appreciation of work is not confined to it. He insists that a monk must work even when he is not compelled to do so by need.

His conception of work as a day in, day out affair is evident in the example he gives of an isolated hermit. This man lived too far from a market to make selling baskets profitable, and in any case he had no need of the money that this would normally have brought in, because he was able to support himself with the vegetable garden which he cultivated. Despite this, he ful-filled his daily basket-making quota, storing his baskets up in a shed, and then at the end of the year he burnt the lot, pur-chased fresh raw material, and started all over again.

Customarily, however, work is tied to the need to earn one's daily bread. Cassian is greatly impressed by the example of St. Paul and he quotes the apostle's advice to the busybodies of Thessalonica: "We enjoin all such, and we urge them strongly in the Lord Jesus Christ, to earn the food they eat by working quietly" (2 Thessalonians 3:12). People who are busy earning their keep have no time to be restless and nosy, and are less inclined to be envious of the gifts and benefits others enjoy. They are also less likely to soar away from the daily grind into the daydreams acedia conjures up. Work, in other words, is a cure for acedia and a vaccination against infection.

Why the therapy works

Why? I think the answer is that work grounds an individ-ual in the nitty-gritty reality of the here and now. Acedia is characterized by a de-temporalization which lifts the person above the concrete reality of daily life into dreams of a better place and a more ideal situation. The disconnectedness of ace-dia sets the individual adrift like an untethered balloon. Its victims expend all their energy in escaping from the burden of time. They wander from one thing to another without ever buckling down to anything. When a hermit stays in his cell and does the work that is in front of him, he takes up the burden of time. He accepts the situation to which God has brought him and he embraces the here and now. He burrows down into the moment and passes beyond its confines. By his absorption in the present he makes time fly.

Sadness drowns its victims in a present which lacks an eternal horizon. For its part, acedia separates those it afflicts from day-to-day reality and casts them adrift in a world of might-have-beens and lost opportunities. Sadness de-eternalizes the perspective of those it troubles, while acedia de-temporalizes the point of view of its target group. The two diseases share certain characteristics, but they have different etiologies and call for distinct remedies.

It seems to me, however, that Cassian describes both of them as what we might term "vocational" diseases. They both reflect a discontent with the factual situation in which an individual finds him or herself. In the one case, the present becomes burdensome because of the failure to take account of the eternal dimension, and, in the other, there is a determined effort to avoid really coming to grips with the hard facts of everyday life. But, by our very nature, we are obliged to live in a specific time and place. When we surrender to sadness, we let our hope in our destiny and our trust in God flag. When we fail to resist acedia, we are uttering a fundamental complaint about the specific vocation to which God has called us and the place in which he has asked us to serve. Acedia is a step back from the concreteness of the present and all the multiplicity of detail that the present implies.

Low-grade infections

Few people, I suppose, are as badly crippled by acedia as the monk in the worst "case scenario" with which Cassian illustrates his description of this disease. There certainly are idlers in the world. And these can be so attached to their slothful pattern of life that they are willing to do just about anything to keep the boredom to which they have become accustomed from being upset by energetic newcomers. Yet most instances of infection are not so obvious.

I suspect that acedia is usually experienced as a reluctance to commit oneself fully to one's unique vocation. We accept our calling and go along with it, but at a certain moment we fully realize the implication of the commitment we have made, and at that point we are called upon to say a wholehearted and fully enlightened "amen" to what we initially undertook with a certain degree of naïveté. Acedia holds us back from that second, full commitment. It suspends us between "yes" and "no." We stay where we are, but we do not take root there. Cassian's hermit still gave his desert hut as his mailing address, but that was not really where he expended his energies.

Acedia makes a diocesan priest regret being a priest in this diocese, in this parish, in this depressing mausoleum of a rectory. It makes the overworked contemplative monk sorry that he joined this order or this monastery. It makes the married woman feel hard done by because her fidelity to the love of God and neighbour has put her in this place and time with this husband and these children. Acedia makes its victims complain about what is and keeps them from facing facts. Above all, it prevents them from getting down to the task of working out the vocation to which God has called them in the prosaic flow of ordinary daily life.

Acedia is the dark side of commitment which arises from the realization that "it's come to this." Instead of piercing through time to the open space beyond it, the victims of acedia seek to escape. They compromise a little; they hold back a bit. They live what may seem to be committed lives without real commitment.

The noonday devil knocks

Lay contemplatives should not be surprised to hear the noonday demon scratching at their door, especially if they have been able to arrange their daily life in accord with their contemplative vocation. Sooner or later, whether they have taken on a monotonous job which acts as a kind of interior wall to shut out the noise and focus the mind, or undertaken some quiet creative work that has the same effect, they are going to look up one day and think, like Cassian's hermit, "Surely my life should amount to more than this sterile prayer and this dull routine." Like Marlon Brando's character in *On the Waterfront,* they are going to think, "I could have been a contender. I could have been a somebody!" They are going to realize that they have talents that have been allowed to go to rust and they are going to want to get out there and do something. However, if they follow John Cassian's advice, they will stick to their task. They will stay where God has placed them and do the work that is in front of them. They will root themselves in the present and incarnate their vocation in the prosaic routines of daily life because only by staying put can they make the unique act of faith God asks of them.

7

Vainglory

In the influential catalogue of the passions which Gregory the Great (d. 604) drew up, pride stands apart from the others as their source and inspiration, while vainglory heads the list of its offspring. In later lists vainglory is subsumed under pride and loses its independent status altogether. John Cassian, however, insists on seeing vainglory and pride as two separate diseases, which can be told apart by the distinct set of symptoms each of them displays and by the disparate treatment these symptoms demand. He is well aware, of course, of the close relationship between vainglory and pride.

He emphasizes, for instance, that both of them paradoxically benefit from the monk's advance in virtue. The other passions fade away with time, but vainglory and pride grow stronger as the monk advances toward purity of heart. The better man he is, the more vainglory and pride have to feed on. The virtuous monk is tempted, in fact, to be proud of humility itself, and knowing that he is not proud of it makes him prouder still! Vainglory and pride are like a fine, poisonous powder that sticks to the underside of virtue and rubs off on the fingers. It is very hard to avoid.

Vainglory and pride puff people up at all stages of their spiritual development, but these vices stand at the end of Cassian's list because they lay in wait for the monk who has mastered the other passions and has risen above the conflict with the crude inclinations of lust, gluttony, and avarice. Now, as it were, he must confront the non-relationality of sin, the "for me alone" aspect of it, in all its nakedness. The self-improvement his advance in virtue has brought about has rendered him vulnerable and more in need of God's grace than ever. The question is: Will the "holy" monk admit this?

The nature of vainglory

What is the difference between pride and vainglory? The proud person stands apart from God and the crowd, in a splendid isolation in which he or she glories in the gifts of God as though in fact they are his or her self-generated, rightful possession. The proud need neither God nor anyone else, and they care not a pinch what heaven or earth thinks of them. The vainglorious, on the contrary, care a great deal what others think of them. In fact, they play for the crowd and its applause. Others constitute the mirror in which the vainglorious delight to see themselves reflected. The proud deny God's right of ownership to the gifts he has bestowed upon them. The vainglorious try to usurp some of the glory that these gifts should render to God. They are petty thieves who try to steal "a piece of the action" for themselves. Instead of saying, "Glorify the Lord with me, he has done great things to me," the vainglorious call out in a thousand subtle ways, "Glorify me, I'm great!"

Vainglory "struts its stuff" in stretch limousines and car phones, hair transplants and high fashion dresses, golden washroom keys and bonus flying points. It is no wonder that writers after Cassian were inclined to see vainglory as pride's silly sibling. Vainglory, however, has a multitude of more refined variations. Those who live a hidden life are prone to advertise the fact, and the ascetically inclined can hardly resist letting others know about their austere existence. In fact, in an age that values self-assertion, it is hard to keep vainglory out of our conversation. The rule seems to be, "I assert myself, therefore, I must be taken seriously." Those who don't put themselves forward as self-made winners run the risk of being written off as non-aggressive wimps.

Vainglory's roots

While Cassian does not formally describe the passions in Aristotelian terms of an excess or deficiency of the normal, it does seem legitimate to ask where vainglory has its roots. What good is perverted here? Cassian never explicitly considers this issue, but he does mention in "Conference 5" that someone tempted to fall into sexual licence can be held back by vainglory and public opinion. Vainglory can also help people persevere in their asceticism.

Therefore vainglory may be seen as a perversion of the support derived from group solidarity. Though adhesion to the group may seem to violate our individuality, in fact it is in and through the group that our uniqueness is fostered. We need the support and encouragement of others. In fact, we need their approval. Vainglory exploits this need of the group for its own end. Instead of standing in the group, with the group, and for the group, the vainglorious stand apart from the group and use the group for their own purposes. They find their reward in the "ohs" and "ahs" they extract from others.

As far as God is concerned, though, the vainglorious do not deny that God is the author of their goodness; rather, they usurp for themselves the glory that is his due. Consequently, it seems to me, that at its deepest level vainglory is a refusal to find our fulfilment in God alone. In some foolish way the vainglorious attempt to get something for themselves. They have been promised a "hundredfold," and they want it here and now. Feeding on the virtues that God has granted us, vainglory exposes our fundamental anxiety and our lack of faith to the world.

Vainglory's variations

John Cassian insists that vainglory is multiform, varied, and subtle. The virtuous may grow vain because of the self-satisfaction they take in the austere lives they live, while beginners, for example, may take credit for crass, material things like the beauty of their voice, the elegance of their bearing, or the fact that they come from rich or noble families. Vainglory can lead monks to misjudge their abilities, and deceive them into undertaking feats that are beyond their strength. Vainglory can even send beginners off into a dream world, where they can imagine what might have been if they had stayed in the world instead of nobly accepting a higher call. They may also fantasize about what would happen here and now, if only their great holiness and extraordinary abilities were known to others. To those who spend too much time there, this fantasy land can become far more appealing than the real world of hot sand, scorpions, and monotony.

To illustrate how the desire to be a "somebody" in the eyes of others can penetrate the desert, Cassian tells the story of an older monk who pays a visit to a younger one. The older monk holds back from knocking on the door when he hears a voice within, thinking that the young man is reading scripture or reciting a memorized passage. Curious to know what section of the Bible the monk is meditating on, the older hermit stops to listen. He quickly realizes, however, that the monk is preaching to an imaginary group of catechumens and playing the role of deacon and priest. The "preacher" is obviously greatly embarrassed when his visitor does finally knock on the door and he realizes that his play-acting has been overheard. The older monk, however, wisely laughs off the incident by noting the exact point in the liturgy at which he had arrived.

Cassian uses this story to introduce the oft-heard saying that monks should flee from women and bishops. The point of the remark is that priesthood, by giving a monk the kind of public role he was inclined to daydream about, would take him away from the silence of his cell and the undisturbed quest for true knowledge just as effectively as marriage. Although there were monks who did accept ordination to the priesthood (and John Cassian was one of them), the traditional teaching was that being ordained to the ministry and going about giving conferences distracted the monk from his primary task. It certainly left him exposed to the temptation to cut a figure in the world.

A monk may be able to avoid ordination, but how does he prevent vainglory from becoming a factor in the secrecy of his cell and in the life he shares with his brethren? The temptation to construct vainglorious schemes obviously must be avoided, but the crux of Cassian's advice is to adhere to the common behaviour of the group. In other words, do nothing that makes you stand out. Giving in to the desire to stand out, to be "notable," twists what should be for the glory of God into something for the glory of men.

A modern remedy

Contemplatives in the modern world are as prone to vainglory as their predecessors were. We do not live in a "face-saving" society where what others think of us is absolutely paramount, but the desire to shine in the eyes of others is still quite strong. In fact, the very restrictions of the contemplative life in the world can become marks of pride and one-upmanship. What, after all, is the sense of living a hidden life, if nobody knows about it!

Cassian illustrates his description of vainglory with the amusing story to which I referred earlier, but he does not recommend what seems to me to be the obvious and most effective remedy for this childish vice: humour. Monastic spirituality, which follows the Roman tradition in its admiration for a certain *gravitas,* has always been suspicious of humour and laughter. But if salvation is indeed by grace and not by works, then a certain light-hearted attitude toward our virtues is in order. The admission that we are silly creatures, prone to do even good and noble deeds for the applause of our peers, would help to keep things in proportion, I think. Our virtues, after all, are means that clear away the rubbish of disorder so that we may enter into a closer relationship with God – they are not medals on our chest. And if our human frailty can't help wearing them there and pointing them out to those who pass by, a bit of humour would help us to remember that the medals of which we're so proud are made of tin and, in any case, should be credited to another source altogether.

The incongruity of the vocation to the contemplative life in the world should make it easy for a lay contemplative to laugh at his or her sorry effort to be open to God. But that terrible dust of vanity tends to stick to your fingers no matter what you do! I think the only hope we have is to keep our heads down, and to enjoy the human comedy and the jester's role we play in it. May God have mercy on his foolish children and forgive us our petty theft of the glory that is his due!

8

Pride

The classical delineation of pride is so strongly associated with a freely willed defiance of God that we have difficulty reconciling this picture of the first and principal sin with our own keen awareness of the role that familial, social, and historical influences play in the formation of a human being. We know from the case studies of psychology and from our personal dealings with others that fear and a sense of inadequacy often hide themselves behind a facade of blustering arrogance. We do believe in free will and we do hold people responsible for their behaviour. Nonetheless, when someone insists on being the centre of attention at all times, we are more likely to look for a psychological explanation than a moral one.

This psychological bent makes us uncomfortable, therefore, with an explanation of pride which reduces that stance to a pure and totally free act of the will. We are too aware of the slanted terrain on which all moral decisions are made; none of us stands on perfectly level ground. All of us must exercise our freedom on the slope built up under us by our predecessors, our culture, and the myriad influences that have shaped us, often without our knowledge or consent.

We see sin and crime committed every day. Though we may rightly assess the seriousness of these violations of the moral code, and though our courts may assign punishment in those matters considered socially unacceptable, no one but God can precisely judge an individual's degree of freedom and just how responsible he is for his acts. Our consciousness of the social dimension of sin, therefore, can make it difficult for us to accept the individualistic emphasis that seemed dominant in the past.

For this reason, we have to be careful to remember that, though later authors turned the list of vices into a hierarchy of capital sins and used the catalogue to describe the apartment levels of Hell, for Cassian the passions remain weaknesses to be combatted. Consequently, we have to keep in mind in approaching Cassian that he is describing the spiritual diseases which afflict human beings; he is not assigning seats in Satan's auditorium. Therapy, not guilt, is the issue. Therefore, Cassian's failure to match our own sensitivity to social influences does not negate the value of his analysis. It may be limited and need to be supplemented by the insights of psychology and sociology, but it proceeds in essentially the same direction. Cassian shares with these sciences the desire to discover the roots of these disorders so that appropriate remedies might be prescribed.

Cassian's approach

In his own efforts to analyse these disorders he uses the best diagnostic tool available in his day: the medical approach which endeavours to discover an appropriate treatment for a disease by focusing the physician's attention on the symptoms, origin and progression of an illness. We note, however, that Cassian applies this medical technique to psychological data: he reads the interior condition through exterior signs. While modern psychology does not ignore the phenomena indicating a mental disorder or an emotional disturbance, through one methodology or another it focuses on the client's revelation of the history of disquiet within. The procedure Cassian followed worked well in his situation because monks were encouraged to open themselves to their spiritual masters. The experienced monk, like a good physician, fitted his broad knowledge of the disease to the specifics of the case, and offered counsel. Today we favour more introspective approaches, which actually shift the responsibility for progress from the therapist to the client. This difference in emphasis, however, does not negate the value of Cassian's insights nor bring his teaching into conflict with modern psychology.

His approach, however, is symptomatic and phenomenological. Thus he describes the proud as they appear from the outside. He emphasizes that the proud stand alone. In their arrogance, they need neither God nor other people to confirm them in their sense of self-worth. Pride, in fact, is a radical denial of dependence. While the vainglorious try to siphon off some of the glory owed to God into their own accounts, the proud go all the way and deny him the right to claim credit for anything they possess. The vainglorious stand apart from the crowd, but remain linked to it by their desperate need of its applause; the proud care not a wit what people think. To put it bluntly, pride is the radical expression of non-relationality.

Cassian describes two types of pride. The first he labels *carnal;* it is a rather ridiculous sense of superiority based on material factors, such as good looks, elegance, and ancestry. The second, which he calls *spiritual,* grounds its illusion of uniqueness in the individual's virtue and closeness to God. The first separates the haughty from the human beings who surround them. The second sets them apart from God himself.

The final battle

Although Cassian puts pride at the end of the list, most of the authors who came after him moved it into first place, eventually creating the catalogue of capital sins with which we are familiar. This rearrangement indicates a shift from a practical level to a more theoretical one. We might even be inclined to conclude that the later arrangement is more intelligent and advanced than the one Cassian follows. We have to remember, however, that Cassian's classification is subtle and flexible. If we look closely, we see once again that we must not take the linearity of the list of passions literally. Although the order in which he places the passions highlights the strongest feature of the causal relationship which binds one element to the next, this generational catalogue does not exhaust all that can be said about their interaction. The truth is that lines linking one passion with another run in all directions. Therefore we must not misunderstand the significance of pride's place at the end of Cassian's list.

Cassian puts pride last because it is both the endpoint where non-relationality must be met head on, and the beginning of the downward curve to entanglement in lust and gluttony. It is both the proper battlefield of those who have stormed the heights, and also, paradoxically, the place where delusions of grandeur can entrap the spiritually advanced in the inclinations of the flesh which they thought they had left far behind. In terms of the phenomenological description Cassian favours, pride is the last enemy to be brought low, but it is also the origin of all our troubles, as he is well aware. The list, therefore, bends back on itself like a strip of metal encircling a wooden wheel. It ends where it began and, in an endless cycle, one thing leads to another.

Cassian does not use the metaphor of a besieged city to illustrate the struggle with pride, but I think that it illustrates his conception of the relationship of pride to the other vices rather well. In this scenario, pride is the army which the virtuous confront when they have pushed back the forces specifically aimed at undermining particular virtues. Lust, gluttony, and the rest are one-target battalions. They carry short-range weapons, and when they have been defeated, they abandon the field and leave the way open for the advancing army of virtue. When the virtuous, who have been picking off this vice and that with some ease, come into the open space before the castle, they find the ramparts manned by pride, pride which is not directed against this or that virtue but against virtue as a whole. The other passions, in fact, are merely pride's minions and specific incarnations of its power. They are, as it were, the divisions it sends out to defeat the weak before they can storm the castle.

Oddly enough, once the various vices have been routed and pride alone stands in the way of victory, the allegiance of the attackers comes into question. Have they, in fact, been drawn over to pride's side somewhere along the line? Has the perfection of the self almost unconsciously become the real goal rather than the development of a relationship with the Other?

The Desert Fathers lived in a world permeated with nostalgia for the "strive to be best" ideal of Greek excellence, while we disillusioned mortals of the twentieth century belong to an era gravely aware of the complexity of our motivation and of the psychological forces which unconsciously influence our behaviour. Perhaps for this reason the Desert Fathers were in greater danger than we are of turning the advance toward God into an Olympic event in which vainglory, and eventually pride, figure. With Freud watching over our shoulder, we are unlikely to sit around competing with one another to determine whose ascetical techniques are superior. Vanity itself and the current democratic fashion of appearing to be simple and unassuming may restrain our preening, but there still remains the subtle danger of growing so used to God's gifts that we take them for granted, or worse, as ours by right. We naturally love the good, and so, inevitably, as our life takes on the harmony and peace of virtue, we are inclined to be delighted with our own image. Pride still stalks the virtuous and those blessed by the gift of contemplative prayer. The Pharisee who gave thanks that he was not a sinner like everyone else is not really so strange a figure as we like to pretend.

Love and humility

Since Cassian sees sin as separation from God and neighbour, and purity of heart as synonymous with love itself, it follows in his view of things that perfection defines a dependent relationship faithfully lived, rather than a mountain successfully climbed. Spiritual advancement is not the result of faithfully following some sort of strenuous self-development program for spiritual athletes. Spiritual progress implies growth in love of God and neighbour. The struggle against the passions is for the sake of love. Perfection considered as a goal in itself is a solitary, isolating, and highly competitive thing. It feeds pride. Perfection considered as a gift is the by-product of love received and reciprocated. It is a tribute to the Other rather than the self. In fact, it has no meaning or value except in terms of love.

Cassian's answer to the problem of pride is to emphasize the importance of seeing our progress in virtue, and even our effort to advance in virtue, as the product of God's grace. If Christ, he asks, confessed that he could do nothing without the Father (John 5:19, 30), then who are we to presume that we can move forward on our own? In his effort to challenge Augustine's dark view of original sin, Cassian got himself into some hot water by appearing to overemphasize human freedom, but he makes it perfectly clear in his treatment of pride that we always owe everything to the mercy of God.

The defeat of pride is obviously impossible without humility. But what does humility mean to Cassian? Our familiarity with the notion that vice is an excess or lack of something properly valued in moderation has conditioned us to think of pride as an excessive love of self and to think of humility, therefore, as a just assessment of one's worth, or simply as "truth." I believe that Cassian's understanding of both pride and humility is slightly different. If he sees pride essentially as an insistence on standing alone, it follows that he perceives humility fundamentally as an acceptance of relatedness. The humble admit their dependence on God and their need of other people. This is perfectly in accord with our earlier perception that the final goal of asceticism and prayer, which is purity of heart, is synonymous with love itself. In other words, the target is not the attainment of some sort of "personal best" to be gloried in, but a relationship to be lived. The self is not what matters! The humble admit this; the proud do not.

Carnal pride

The spiritually proud become so enamoured with their own goodness that they tend to forget that they owe it to God who has rescued them from the isolation of sin. Once these sinners are on their feet, as it were, and fortified with virtue, they distance themselves from the divine physician and take personal credit for the strength they feel. Those who are subject to what Cassian calls "carnal pride" are in a somewhat different position. They never really surrendered themselves to the relationship in the first place. Their pride keeps them from letting go of whatever it is that makes them special.

These poor souls retain a sense of being separate from the other brethren. Inevitably, avarice takes root in them as they assume personal charge of their own security. In addition, their illusion of superiority makes them disobedient, hard and uncooperative. They join up, as it were, but never really belong, because they are better than the rest, after all. In time, acedia is added to the list of vices in which their non-commitment has entangled them.

These early victims of pride lack the haughty reserve of the "perfect." They are loud, talkative, extraordinarily joyful or, on the contrary, spectacularly morose, sad, and bitter. Whatever their mood, it is meant to attract attention. Wherever they are and however they feel, they assume centre stage as their inherent right.

In his treatment of these early victims of pride, Cassian remarks that, in order to treat our weaknesses, we must first know their origin and cause. The fact is, however, that though we may be impressed by his effort to penetrate to the root of the problem in his exploration of each passion, what really convinces us that Cassian knows what he is talking about are his phenomenological descriptions of the victims of the various passions. We know he is on to something, because these people whose psychological ancestors troubled the quiet of the Egyptian desert inhabit the office towers of the modern city and are well known to all of us.

For instance, if we strip the proud monk of his habit, put him in a business suit and secularize the context, Cassian's description of this weary individual's discomfort at being trapped in a spiritual conference has a modern ring to it. He sits there playing with his fingers and fidgeting as though he has fleas, wondering all the while what he, a spiritual giant, who should be an abbot or a hermit storming the heights, is doing marooned among these amateurs. He is quick to take offence and to think that he is the personal target of any critical remarks. He can be belligerent and just as quickly tumble over into sadness. He is caught in a no-win situation. He refuses to apologize for any insult that he may have uttered in the heat of discussion, and if someone tries to placate him by offering him an apology for any imagined wrong, he grows indignant at this display of humility.

Full circle

We have come full circle. Cassian's proud individual is walking the familiar paths of avarice, acedia and anger. As much as anything, Cassian's examples demonstrate that, though he puts pride at the end of his list, he recognizes it as the cause and origin of all our troubles.

Humility, understood as a rightly ordered relationship to God and neighbour, is in Cassian's opinion a reliable bulwark against pride. The test of the authenticity of this humility is a monk's obedience to the elders and his readiness to die to the world. If humility is the acceptance of relatedness, not surprisingly it is a virtue which we cannot cultivate without the help of others. For example, Cassian mentions the importance of having guides who clearly witness to the fact that they owe whatever spiritual advancement they have achieved to faith rather than their labour.

He mentions that their purity, which we can legitimately describe as their at-oneness-with-God, causes them to lament even the little sins which are impossible to avoid. They are keenly aware of the distance between the purity for which they yearn, and the purity they possess. Clearly, for these individuals virtue is a matter of relationship, rather than a spiritual perfection that parallels some gymnastic achievement. In fact, without the horizon of the Other, virtue itself is merely a neater, more socially accepted form of the self-centredness sloppily represented by drunkenness and fornication.

Cassian concludes his study of pride by recommending an "I am the least of my brethren" attitude as a prophylactic against infection. I think that we should see this as a restraint on our readiness to rise up indignantly against the little annoyances and putdowns that are a feature of daily life. He is not advocating an obsessive preoccupation with the "unworthy self." Obsessive humility is merely pride using an alias. In the same vein, Cassian suggests that keeping in mind the shortness of our time on this earth will help us to keep life's ups and downs in proportion. In all things, he reminds us, we need to remember that we can do nothing without God. This is so thoroughly true that even being able to grasp this perception is, itself, a gift of God!

Conclusion

In the fifth century, monks and bishops in the south of France prodded John Cassian to record his memories of the Egyptian desert, so that they might benefit from the wisdom of those who stood in an ascetical tradition stretching back to St. Anthony himself. Since then, century after century, monks have mined his *Institutions* for wisdom to live by. Their reading has not been motivated by their curiosity about the past, but by their desire to find an answer to the question of how to be faithful to their calling in their own time and place.

We have read a section of this fifth-century work with the same question in mind: What does this text, which encapsulates a tradition stretching back to the very beginnings of Christian contemplative life, have to say to those who are attempting to live contemplative lives today? What does it have to say to us, here and now? We have asked, in particular, whether it has anything to offer men and women in the midst of the world who withdraw to the edge of things, without fanfare or recognition, quietly to pursue lives of solitude, prayer and study. Can a work written by a lover of the eremitic life be of any use to married and single men and women, persons who defy the standard notion that lay people are oriented toward the world, and action in it, by opting for a life of prayer?

In this study we have sat at the feet of a spiritual master, as it were and, as was customary in the desert, we have asked him for a "word" by which we might guide our lives. As Cassian has described the disorders and propensities within us which keep us from being fully, calmly, and spontaneously focused on God, we have tried to see how these analyses of the "passions," based as they are on an ancient, experiential wisdom expressed in the diagnostic terminology of medicine, apply to us today. We have noted that, though Cassian pays no explicit attention to the psychological and sociological factors that are so important to us, his use of the notion of disease to describe the passions or vices in fact does leave room for the inclusion of all the positive and negative influences which have made us who we are. Cassian's practical, "country doctor" approach to the pressures which push us this way and that creates a horizon within which the insights of modern psychology can be situated. His concern, however, is not so much how we got to be the way we are, in some sort of Freudian sense, but how we can co-operate with grace to overcome our disabilities and become fully responsive to God's love.

One of the biggest barriers to hearing Cassian has been our familiarity with the use to which later generations have put revised versions of the list of passions he employs. In fact, we tend to think of them as "capital sins" or "bad habits" that need to be identified, noted, and checked off, one by one, as they go down in defeat before our indomitable will. We tend to think of them as moral faults for which we are fully responsible. We have seen, however, that Cassian's notion of "disease" makes his list of passions broader, more inclusive, and far more subtle than the speculative classification of sins that students in catechetical classes once rhymed off by rote.

A second factor hindering our reception of what John Cassian has to say to us today has been our deeply ingrained presumption that the whole ascetical tradition which he represents was dominated by a Greek-inspired hatred of the body which we are proud to have moved beyond. We have seen that in reality John Cassian neither hates the body nor sets himself up as some kind of highly qualified spiritual gymnast who can teach us to transcend the flesh. His approach is thoroughly therapeutic and amusingly down to earth. We have noted time and again that he sees us as damaged human beings whose progress in sanctity requires a healing of the defects which inhibit our freedom.

What he describes, in fact, is the process of faithfully living out our baptismal commitment. The Holy Spirit summons us to a purity of heart which enables us to respond spontaneously to all that happens to us in terms of our relationship to God. This is not something we can proudly achieve on our own. In fact, only God can rewire us, as it were, so that unselfish love, rather than egocentric concupiscence, is our intuitive response.

Cassian's study offers us a guide to the good health that purity of heart represents. Despite its practical tone and its examples that ring as true today as they did so many centuries ago, his book nonetheless stands in the same relationship to an individual's particular situation as a textbook description of a disease does to a specific case. We are not dealing here with abstractions or with theology as a science: the issues are practical, and the applications individual and unique. As we have seen, the outline Cassian offers us is helpful and timely. It still remains true that each person would be wise to seek a spiritual guide to apply this general knowledge to his or her particular situation.

Blessed indeed are those lay contemplatives lucky enough to find a qualified spiritual counsellor who can understand their needs and minister to them! Blessed, in any case, are those who can sit at the feet of John Cassian and absorb the wisdom of the men and women who went out into the Egyptian desert seeking wholeness, health and God.

For Further Reading

Anson, Peter F. *The Call of the Desert*. London: SPCK, 1973.
See esp. pp. 8-53.

Brown, Peter. *The Body and Society: Men, Women and Sexual Renunciation in Early Christianity*. New York: Columbia University Press, 1988. For a sympathetic introduction to the life experience and aspirations of the hermits in the Egyptian desert, see pp. 213-240.

Chadwick, Owen. *John Cassian: A Study in Primitive Monasticism*. Cambridge: Cambridge University Press, 1950.

Chitty, Derwas James. *The Desert a City: An Introduction to the Study of Egyptian and Palestinian Monasticism under the Christian Empire*. Oxford: Blackwell, 1966.

The Lives of the Desert Fathers: The Historia Monachorum in Aegypto. Translated by Norman Russell. *Cistercian Studies Series, 34*. London: Mowbray, 1981.

The Sayings of the Desert Fathers: The Alphabetical Collection. Translated by Benedicta Ward. *Cistercian Studies Series, 59*. London: Mowbray, 1975.

INNER JOURNEY SERIES

BROTHER FIRE, SISTER EARTH
The Way of Francis of Assisi
for a Socially Responsible World

Adela DiUbaldo Torchia

Adela Torchia shows us why Saint Francis is still so very important for anyone
trying to remain faithful to Christ's gospel today.
ISBN 2-89088-617-4
80 pages, 5.25 x 8.25 inches, $7.95

HEALING THE HEART
Desert Wisdom for a Busy World

Kenneth C. Russel

Author Kenneth C. Russell has us sit symbolically at the feet of John Cassian,
one of the Desert Fathers and spiritual master to ask him, as was customary in
the desert, for a "word" by which we might guide our lives today.
ISBN 2-89088-618-2
96 pages, 5.25 x 8.25 inches, $7.95

KNOWING THE GOD OF COMPASSION
Spirituality and Persons Living with AIDS

Richard P. Hardy

Author Richard Hardy lets people with AIDS tell their story; and, in so doing,
their way of being religious, their way of coming to know the God of compas-
sion, unfurls before you.
ISBN 2-89088-632-8
80 pages, 5.25 x 8.25 inches, $7.95

TO ORDER

Novalis
49 Front Street East, Second Floor, Toronto, ON M5E 1B3
1 -800-387-7164
Toronto area (416) 363-3303
1-416-363-9409